I0475298

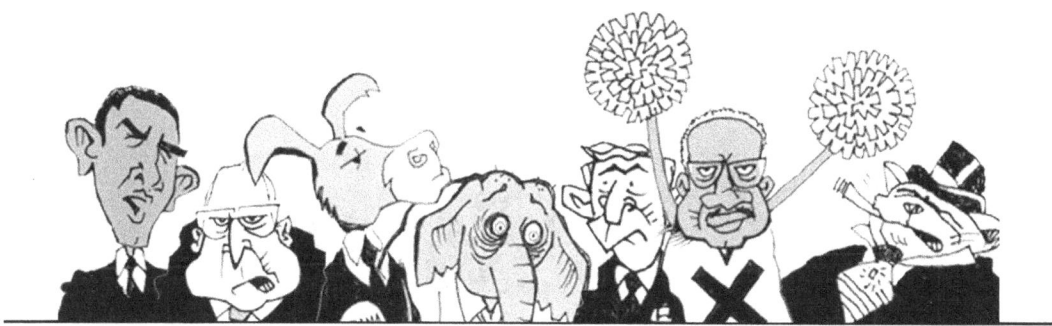

bush's nose

retooned in *The Durango Telegraph 2002-2010*
with selected cartoons from *The Huffington Post*

All illustrations & annotations ©2010 by Shan Wells

"Long Before Twitter and Facebook"©2010 by Bob Cesca
"Shan Wells and the Art of Political Cartooning"©2010 by Judith Reynolds
"Yes"©2010 by Paul Gibbons

www.shanwells.com/cartoon

ISBN: 978-1456346065
First Edition 2010 A B C D E
Printed in the United States of America

Published by Illuminati Press

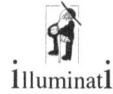

illuminati

THE BROADCAST NEWS LINE-UP:

JOURNALISTS

PUNDITS

HACKS

FUCKING BATSHIT

PBS · MSNBC · CBS · CNN · FOX

SHAN©09
durango telegraph

Contents

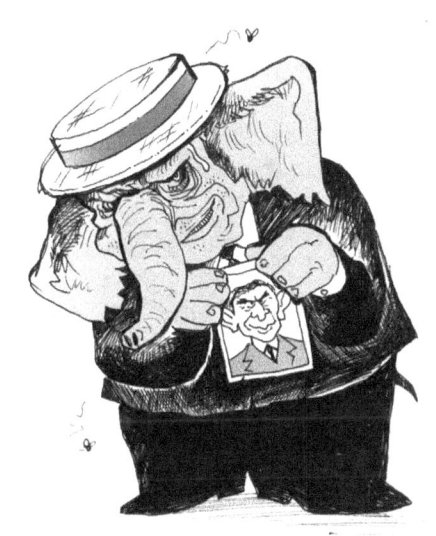

Nose.

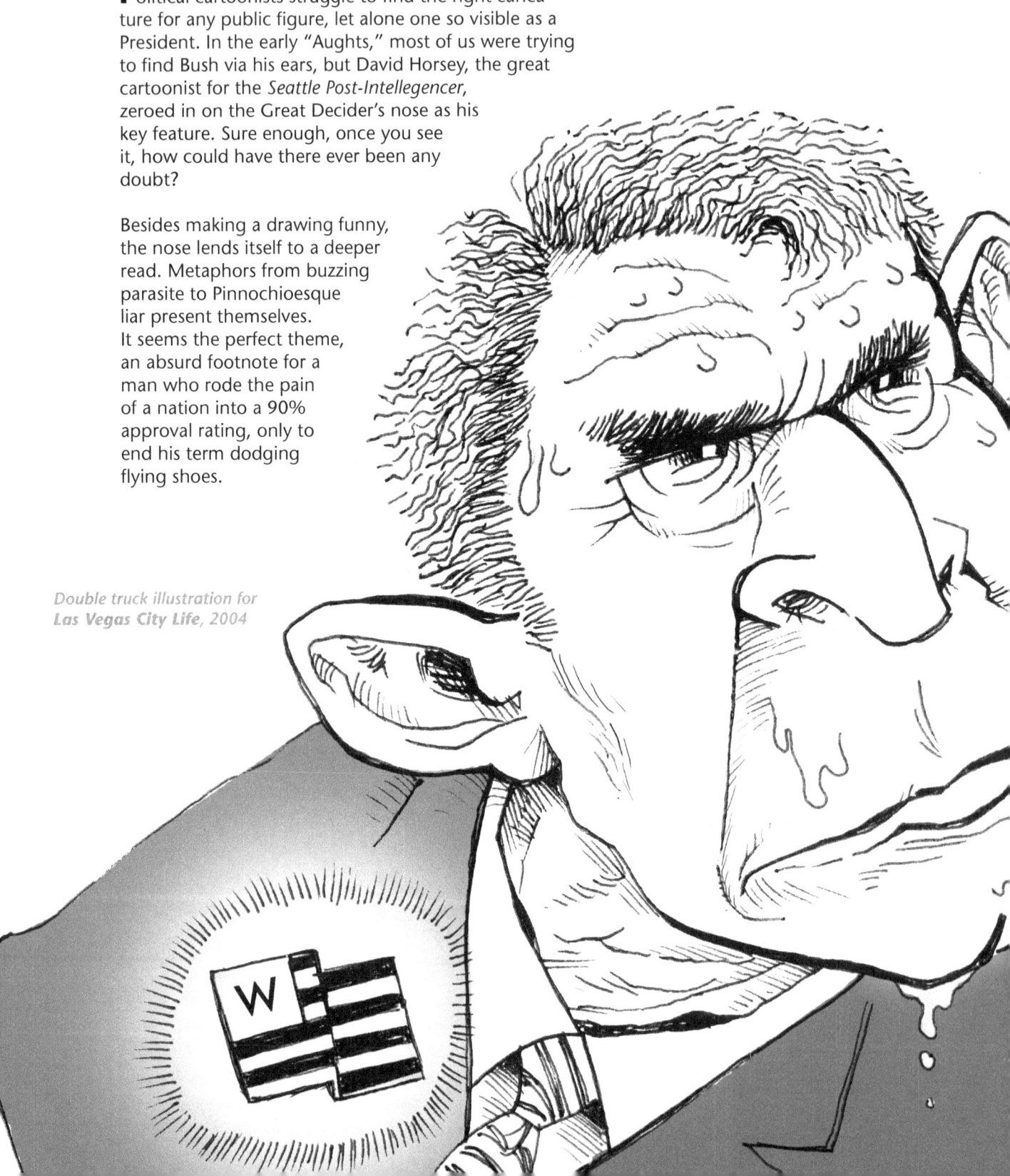

Political cartoonists struggle to find the right caricature for any public figure, let alone one so visible as a
President. In the early "Aughts," most of us were trying
to find Bush via his ears, but David Horsey, the great
cartoonist for the *Seattle Post-Intellegencer*,
zeroed in on the Great Decider's nose as his
key feature. Sure enough, once you see
it, how could have there ever been any
doubt?

Besides making a drawing funny,
the nose lends itself to a deeper
read. Metaphors from buzzing
parasite to Pinnochioesque
liar present themselves.
It seems the perfect theme,
an absurd footnote for a
man who rode the pain
of a nation into a 90%
approval rating, only to
end his term dodging
flying shoes.

Double truck illustration for
***Las Vegas City Life**, 2004*

Metatoon

In the bright, shiny new year of 2000, my wife Regina and I had just returned from New Zealand. After two years down under, America was much changed to our eyes. There was more Christian proselytizing in television and radio shows. The radical right wing was surprisingly visible, and even the left seemed bitter about 8 years of Clintonesque drama, despite the bubbling economy and a deficit surplus.

I voted Green that year, having been convinced by a consortium of progressive activists that Al Gore was much the same as G.W. Bush. When a divided Supreme Court crowned the man from Texas king, I reckoned there would not be too much drama. George W. was obviously not that bright and would probably only last one term, like his dad.

Ten years, two wars, one terrorist attack, and an economic melt-down later, Bush holds a place in American history that will be remembered as one of our darkest periods. Instead of inspiring unity, the Administration became a secretive fortress of partisanship, willing bend or break any law necessary to underwrite a neoconservative, neocolonial agenda.

I watched, wrote and protested, but W.'s presidency made a furrow in my life that demanded planting. Perhaps it was my latent guilt at having contributed, however infinitesimally, to W.'s election by making the perfect the enemy of the good. I needed to do more than rant in letters to the editor and march with a bloodstained placard. When an opportunity to create political cartoons came, I seized it.

Ironically, I'm therefore grateful to Bush. Without him, I, and a surprising large number of others would have done something different with our lives. Dubya forced a championing of progressive beliefs that led directly to the historical election of 2008. Just as few in 1999 could have predicted the train wrecked 2000's, even fewer would have guessed our next president would be a black liberal intellectual with a Muslim name.

Such convoluted spasms of hubris followed by ideological resurgences and counter-resurgences are one of the most fascinating things about following American politics. Our ability for reinvention is limited only by our capacity to forget. Even as I write this, barely 20 months into a new presidency built upon a burned out Bushy husk, the damage done by that administration is being smoothed over. Already the right wing, newly reincarnated as the Tea Party, is serving up a dose of generational amnesia, blaming all our country's current woes on the guy now in office, instead of on the man whose policies ravaged three countries.

A documentation of that damage, this book accounts a small bookmark for future generations who will surely ask why we went to war in Iraq, why the largest financial collapse since the Great Depression occurred on Bush's watch, and why so many had to be sacrificed for the money, ambition and corrupt power he unleashed, perhaps unwittingly.

This work is dedicated to the memory of those lost, and to the edification of those to come. Judge us, you unborn. Weigh our actions as your forebears. Remember, though, you too will be confronted with such things. You too will be asked to respond, with history taking notes and clicking her salty tongue.

Long Before Twitter and Facebook.

Bob Cesca

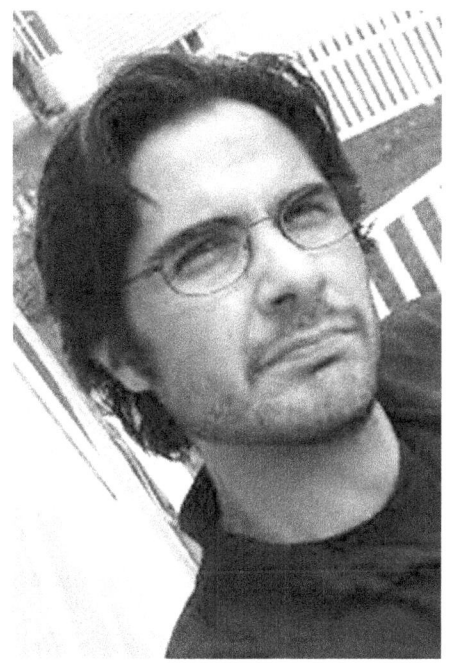

Bob Cesca is an American director, producer, writer, actor, blogger and political commentator.

Cesca writes weekly columns in The Huffington Post, which he has written since August 2005.He's also a weekly columnist for AOL's WalletPop blog.

Cesca grew up in Washington, D.C. and Northern Virginia. He graduated from Kutztown University of Pennsylvania with a Bachelor's degree in Political Science. In his personal life, Cesca is an avid bicycling fan. He estimates that he rides between 50 and 100 miles a week.

About Cesca, Cenk Uygur of The Young Turks has said that "Bob's writing is totally fearless. That's what I love about it."

Long before Twitter and Facebook, political cartoonists were absolutely the first "micro-bloggers." The ability to express ideas and satire in the 2000s requires a quick wit and instantly cutting analysis. Political cartoonists have always been on the vanguard of this form of social expression. One panel. Limited words. And fearless, kinetic artwork. The economy of a concise idea and the creative chops required to illustrate those ideas are at the center of what it means to be an effective political cartoonist.

In so many ways, Shan Wells defines what political cartoons are all about. His work is instantly iconic. His illustrations stand alone and are purely original in a genre overloaded with copycats and knockoffs.

With a daily onslaught of information – scandals, controversies, and media overload – it's sometimes easy to forget about the events that have shaped America in 2011. Shan's panels, as collected in this anthology, provide an utterly subversive history of the first decade of the 21st Century. A wicked counterpoint to the stories told by the corporate press and cable news talkers. It's a history that's as crucial, if not more so, than the official line pumped into the mainstream by glad-handers and well-paid media shills.

Shan's work will make you laugh and it will make you cringe – and it might even piss you off, recalling long forgotten news flashes all over again. Of course, these are the reactions you're supposed to experience when viewing truly great political commentary. So hang on tight and pass along what you read here: the micro-history of America as told by a rare and talented artist.

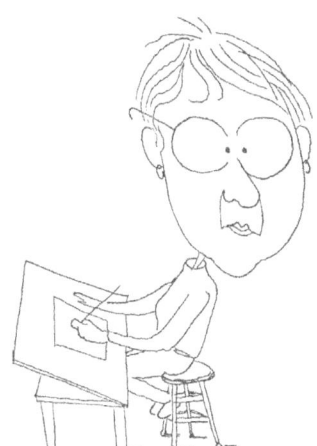

Shan Wells and the Art of Political Cartooning

Judith Reynolds

Judith Reynolds is a journalist and political cartoonist for The Durango Herald whose assignment is local issues.

Following graduate work in art history at the University of Michigan, Reynolds embarked on a teaching career but eventually migrated to the messier, muddier, and more challenging fields of journalism and contemporary cultural commentary.

Shan Wells has never lost his edge. Not since he first started speaking his mind in a public forum a decade ago. His political cartoons have ranged over the foothills of his hometown to the bloody borders in the Middle East. And he has never lost his edge – or his nerve.

That's the highest compliment one political cartoonist can pay to another. Add high marks for conceptual development and strong execution, and you have a young American satirist following in the footsteps of the great Thomas Nast.

Like every political cartoonist, Wells takes aim at the foibles of human-kind. He does so with ferocity and precision. His understands how and how often hypocrisy is at play in the world. He's clear and present, as clear as Daumier was in the nineteenth century or the éminence gris of American cartooning today -- Pat Oliphant. Wells' notion of human foolhardiness is never in doubt. And his anger at outright mendacity takes shape in his astonishing imaginary dramas.

The trick with political cartooning, of course, is to spring from an angry mind and be comprehensible. Wells' twin gift as a writer may be hidden, but it's there in every box under the banner: ReTooned/by Shan Wells.

Political cartoonists dispatch cantankerous opinions with a pen dipped in passion and commitment. Some succeed, others don't. Not every cartoonist has the right tools at his or her disposal. There are plenty with good ideas but only a limited understanding of visual symbols. There are more with tepid ideas or weak powers of visualization who happen to have splendid drawing skills. Wells is a lucky guy; he has everything – clear ideas, telling visual metaphors, and superb drawing skills.

In 2010 he has simplified dramatic scenes to a few essential characters -- Uncle Sam falling in defeat over health care reform or a map shattered to pieces by a Supreme Court ruling. Leaving backgrounds uncluttered, Wells focuses on the principal actors, often in opposition to each other, to drive home a point.

In one of his most successful Tea Party cartoons, he skillfully staged a parade with a small loud-mouth in front being manipulated behind the scenes by a Republican Party elephant and more important, a fat, arch-conservative cat from Wall Street. In another about the mosque controversy at Ground Zero, Wells has reduced the conflict to one American Muslim facing an angry trinity: a Tea Party Republican, a Westboro Baptist preacher, and a hooded KKK member carrying a burning cross. Together they angrily shout: "You can't build near Ground Zero because your religion is all about hate."

Lest anyone think developing a potent scene like that is easy, try it.

May you never lose your edge, Shan.

YES

Paul Gibbons

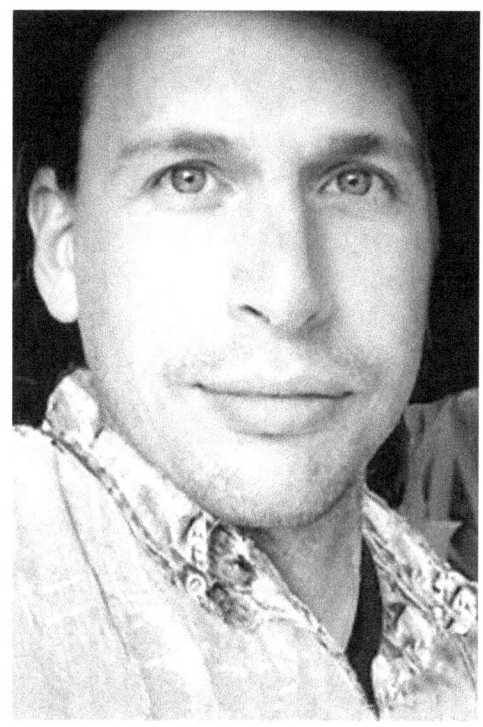

Underneath the heavy radioactivity of satire and rant, a political cartoon asks us to confront this question: what side are you on? But take a collection of cartoons that span four or more years, and you have a reconstruction that goes beyond the binary -- it's an analog, hand-drawn, old-school history full of nuance and subtle cunning, of degrees and blended value like a color palette that shifts its tones when you take it into the sun and back to shade again. The question then is not centered so much on whose side you've taken and loved (X's or Y's) but how those battle lines have shifted and where those soldiers are now.

As of the printing of this book, Hillary Clinton has relieved us of the well-illustrated baggage surrounding Condeleeza Rice's tenure as secretary of state. The right-wing ideology flushed down the political toilet has been resurrected as group of self-serving, down-home, constitution-loving, plain-speaking 'mericans who take their party's name from an act of defiance against the British Empire in the 18th century. Karl Rove has focused on garnering speaker fees from any institution that wants to hear The Real Story of the Great Bush Years That The Media Still Refuses to Tell. Bush has been -- well, what has he been up to?

Paul Gibbons is the author of the chapbook Bray (Elixir Press, 2008). His work has appeared in numerous journals, including Beloit Poetry Journal, The Massachusetts Review, Bateau, and The Journal.

Gibbons received the 2006 Rainmaker Award from Zone 3 Press. He teaches at the University of California, Merced.

Hereby hang the tales: from these pages of cartoons, we're more sensitive now to the idiot-ology of those whose first passion is service to the corporate raider in the guise of evangelical, true worshippers of some one true faith. We've experienced the pulling back of the veil of Fox News. We've seen what happens when elected officials pretend it's not their job to be leaders who can speak clearly and compassionately both domestically and abroad.

Personally, Shan Wells' collection also makes me wonder whether his cartoons as a body of work will be most remembered for pointing out the political and social idiocies we've witnessed over four years or so, or whether the leap of associations we make will be more to the artistry -- will we say, "Yeah, I remember that time when such and such lied to all of us," or will we say, "You know, those were damn good cartoons"?

Our reactions, surely, will be as nuanced and shaded as ourselves. For each of us, we will enter an incomplete, analog sense we get when looking at the illustrations from page to page -- the binary invisible and forgotten as we hold this book in our hands, thumb ready and forefinger licked for turning to the next sharp metaphor, the next exaggerated figure that chronicles our political fortune. And the answer to the question, What side are you on? is ironically one side of a binary: YES. The big YES that keeps me following the movers and shakers closely and critically. I trust that hard-earned YES. I have to. In the long run, it is the only answer that captures the loud and complex laughter I get from these cartoons.

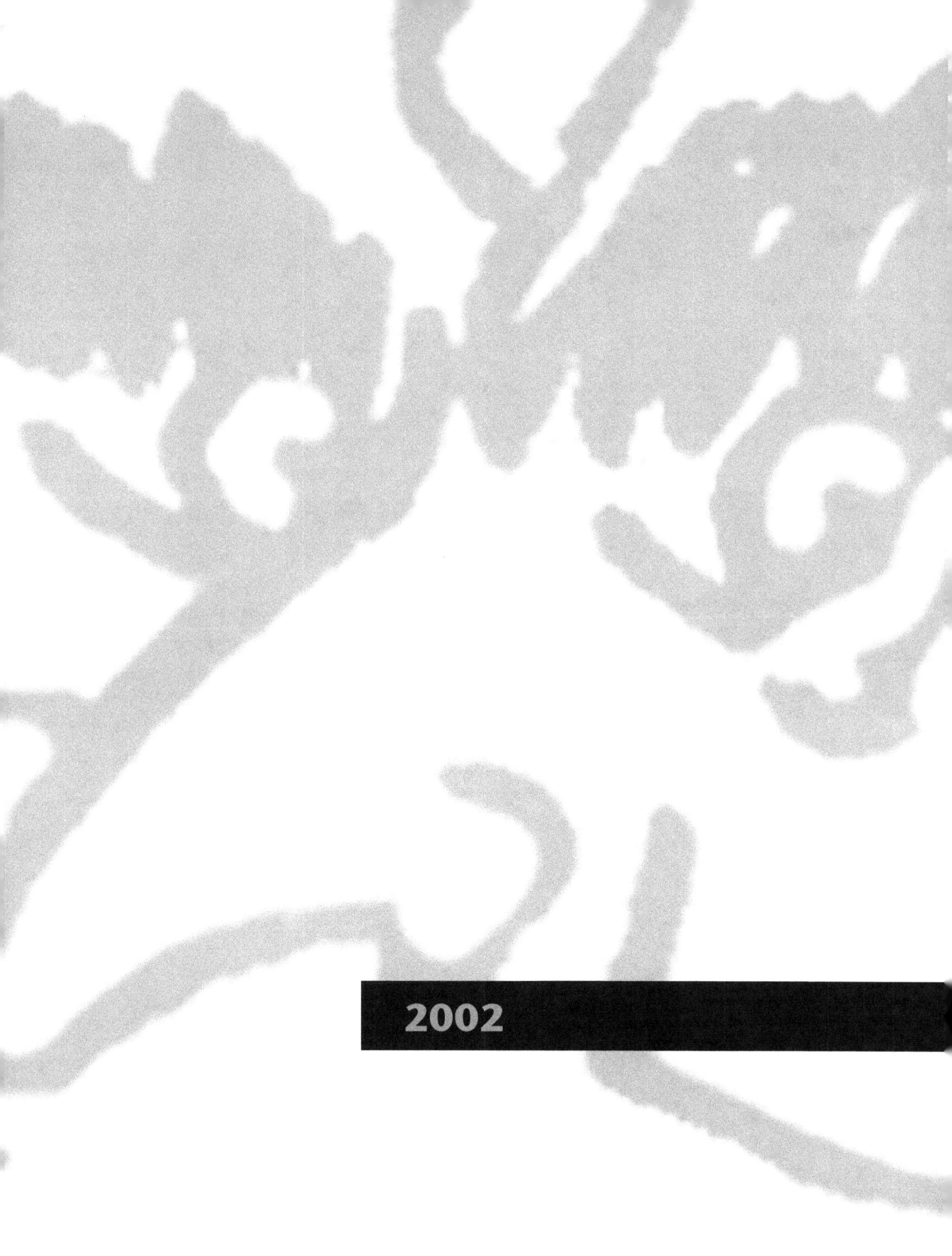

2002

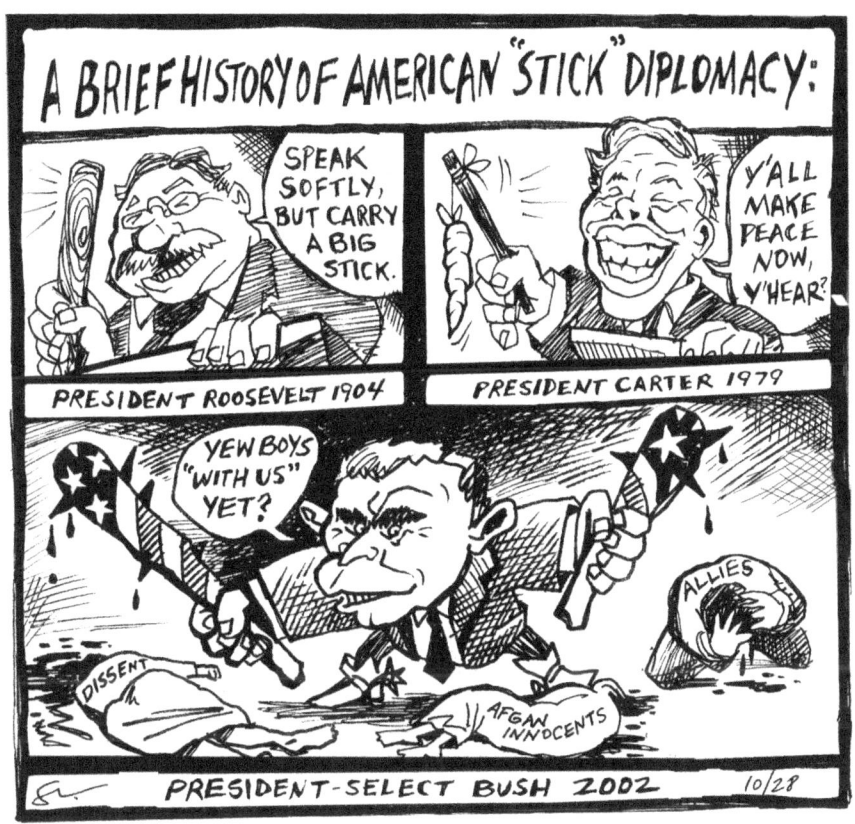

Stick Diplomacy was the first cartoon I made for the *Telegraph*, and it was never published. It was made as an example of what I could do so that *Los Jefes* could determine if I rated a regular column.

At the time, "President-Select" was a term much in vogue, as G.W. Bush had been basically selected by the Supreme Court to be president, having tied with Al Gore in the 2000 election. The mood of cartoon reflects the way many on the left perceived the US Administration- as an overbearing, violent, dangerous force whose idea of diplomacy was literally "you're with us or you're against us."

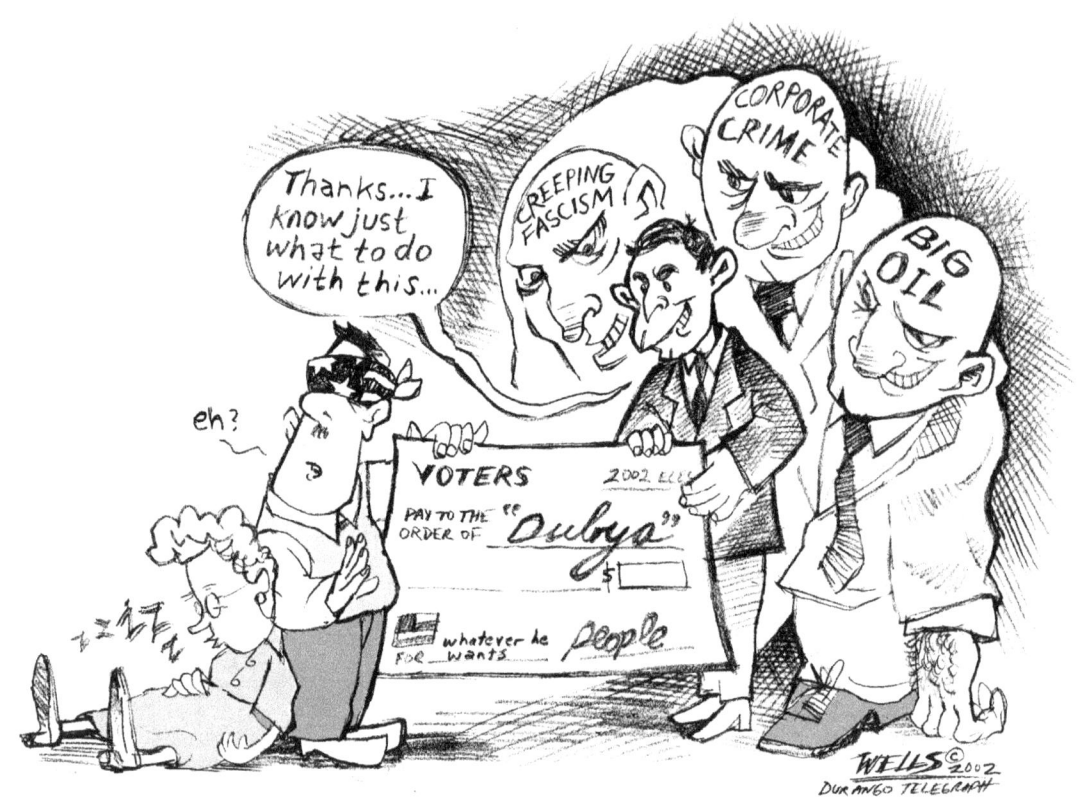

The 2002 mid-term elections swept the Republicans into full control of the Senate, House and Presidency. The ascendant Neo-cons were granted full authority to do their will. Symbolic of the blind patriotism that a majority of Americans displayed when asked to think about our stance in the world, a flag hid the eyes of my Joe Voter. Deregulation and tax breaks for corporations also came front burner with a strengthened GOP.

This work was done entirely with pencil. I was attempting to determine the limits of newspaper reproducibility. Although the cartoon came out fine, I was not happy with the look, and reverted back to pen and ink from then on.

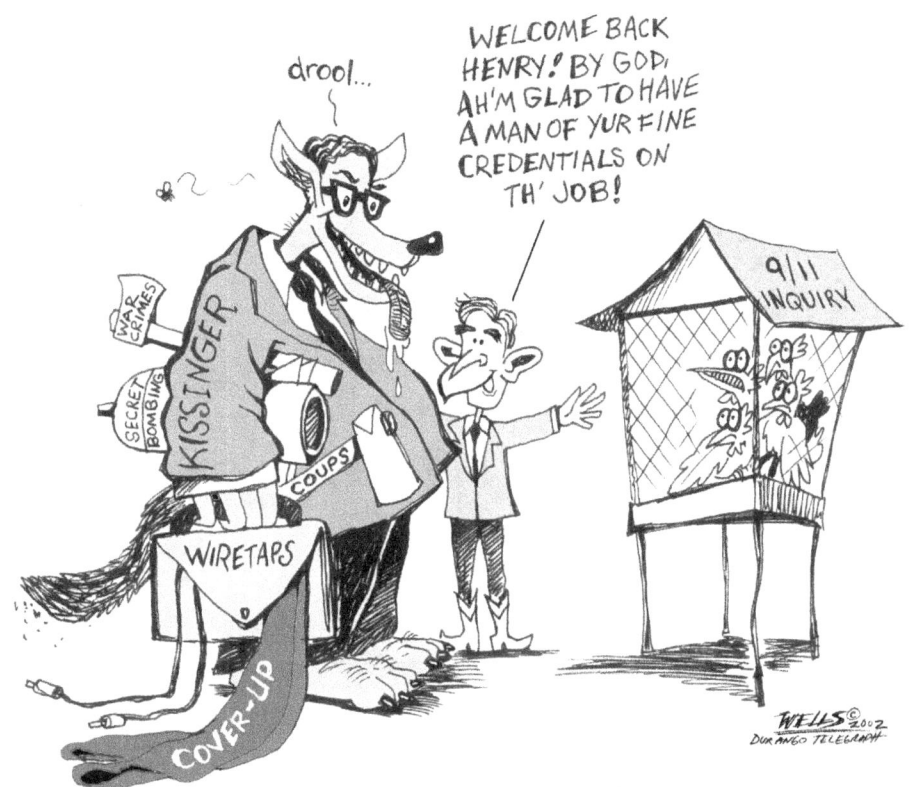

The incredibly weak federal inquiry into 9/11 was capped with the appointment of none other than Henry Kissinger as chair. Given Dick Cheney's deep identification with Nixon and all things Unitary Executive, this was just too much for any reasonable person. The obvious metaphor was the fox and the henhouse.

At this point I was still using my last name for a signature, and settled on big cowboy boots for Bush, a convention I would keep until 2004.

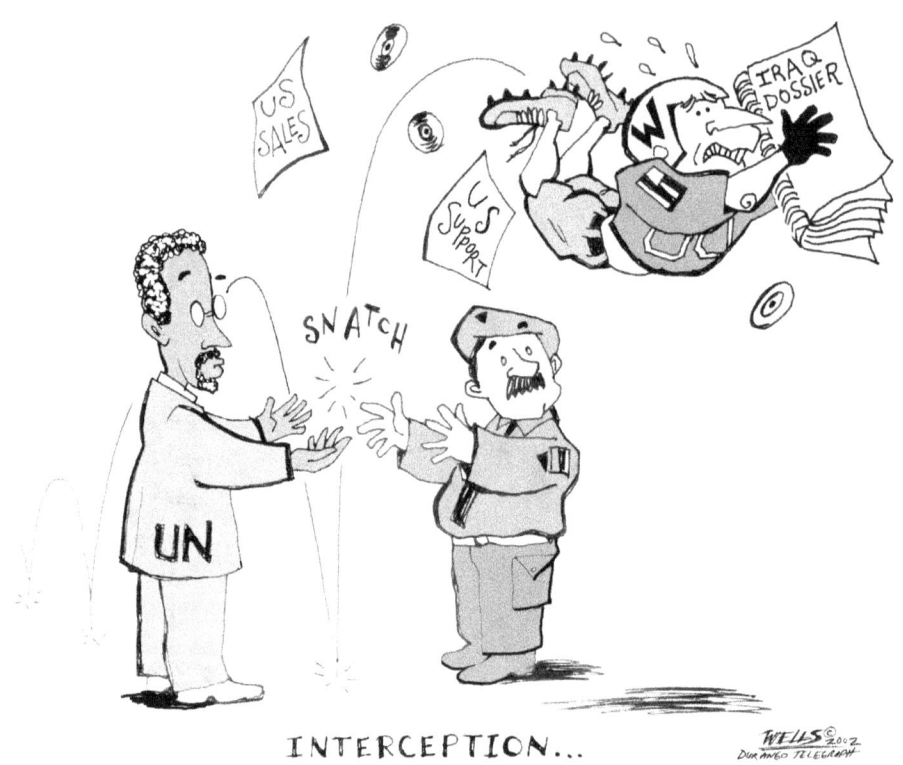

INTERCEPTION...

The Iraq dossier was an 11,807 page hot potato that outlined in detail Iraq's WMD capability as required by the UN. It included information about the chemical weapons and covert support sold or given to Iraq by the U.S. One of the key pre-war demands of the United States was that Iraq turn over the dossier.

Playing about the only card he could, Hussein turned the document over to the U.N., where it was immediately snatched up by the State Department and taken away, on the ludicrous pretext that the U.N. was unable to photocopy it efficiently. More likely, the Administration wanted to make sure it redacted the documents before distributing them to other member states.

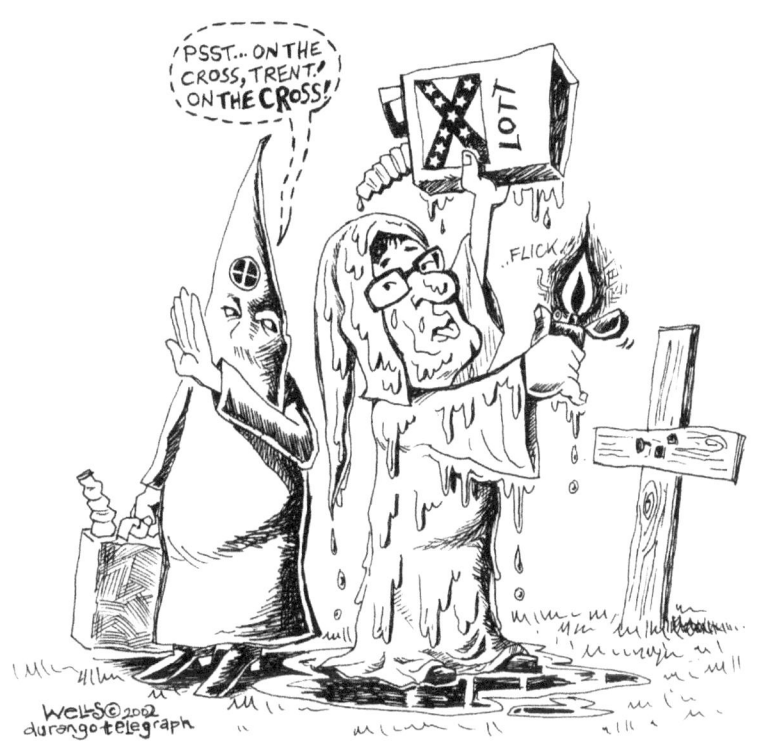

Republican Senate Majority Leader Trent Lott made an unfortunate statement in 2002 at the 100th birthday party for South Carolina Senator Strom Thurmond. He said,

> "When Strom Thurmond ran for president, we voted for him. We're proud of it. And if the rest of the country had followed our lead, we wouldn't have had all these problems over the years, either."

Only problem was, Thurmond ran on a racial segregation platform in 1948. The remark cost him his leadership, and made him a laughing stock nationally.

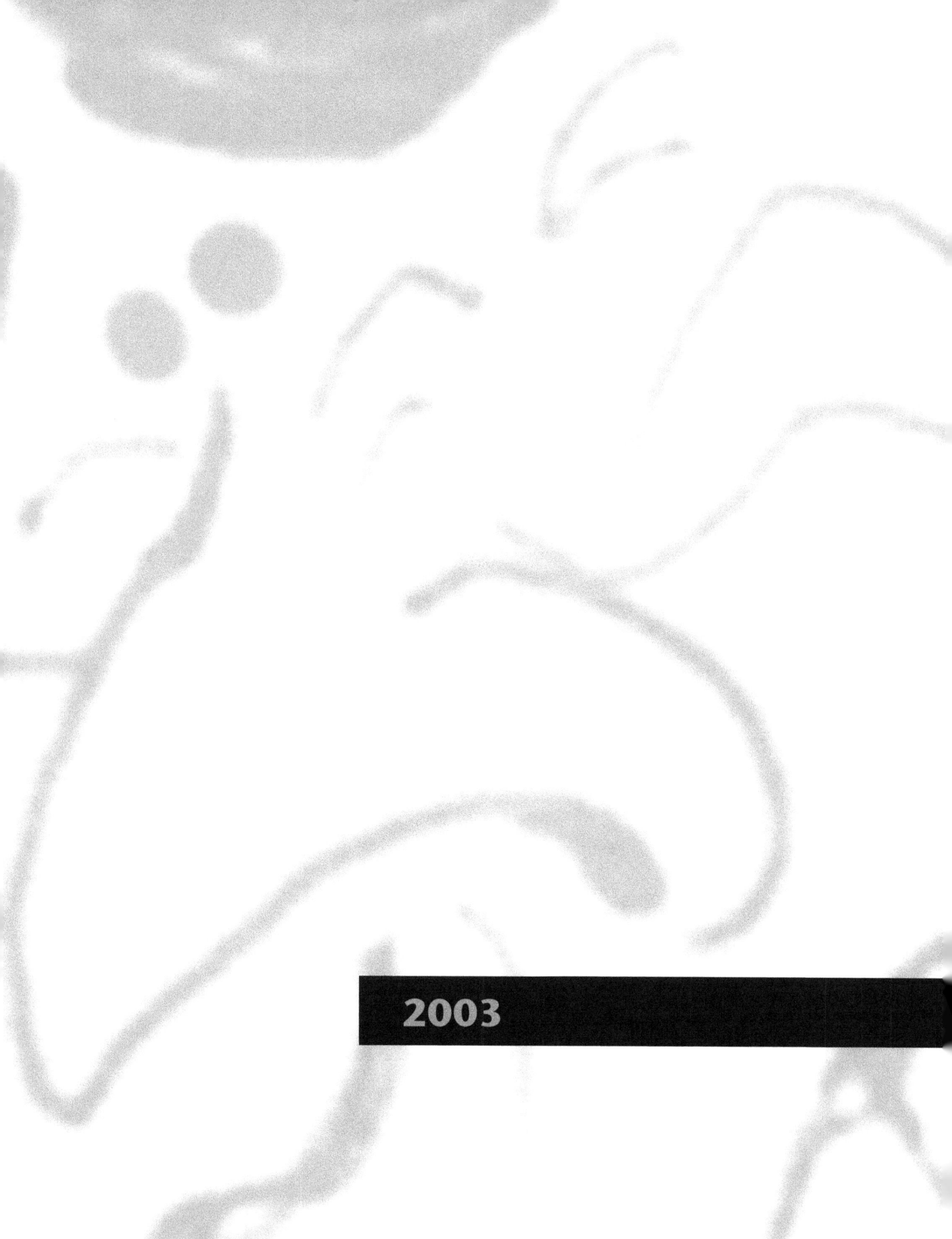

2003

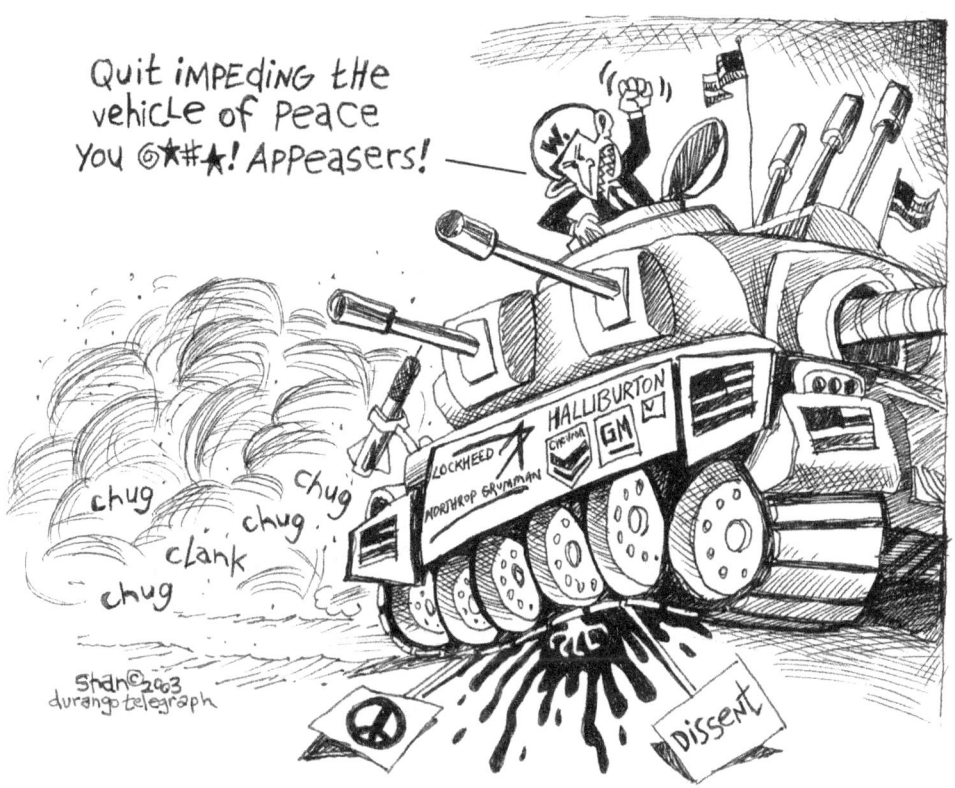

From early on, we folk adamantly against the Iraq War could tell it was going to be a rough ride.

Every President that has ever gone to war has declared it an act of aggression designed to bring about peace, and in some cases that was true. In others, such as Bush's war, it was so blatantly not about anything remotely resembling a just cause that putting sponsor decals on the tank seemed appropriate, given the imperialist profiteering taking place.

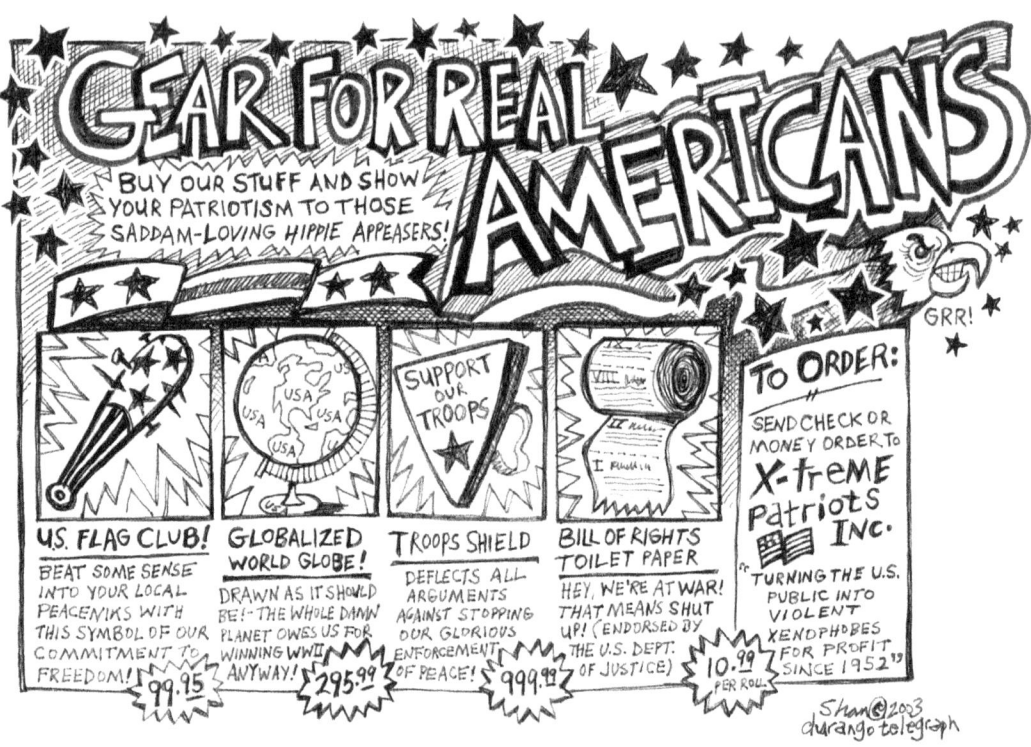

It's hard to describe the intensity of the right's anger against anyone or anything not 110% AMERI-CAN in the early 'Aughts. Faux patriotism ran so rich as to culminate in a Congress passing a resolution changing the name of french fries to "freedom fries" in the Hill commissary as a rather juvenile response to the French refusal to go along with a rush to war.

This cartoon attempted to capture not only the shrill, chest-thumping nonsense that characterized the country's mood, but also the ever-present American "make-a-buck" values that seem to accompany any social movement, parasitizing it and prolonging it by offering ever-more offensive schwagg. It was a purely personal move to make the outline of the cartoon loosely resemble the geographic borders of the United States, with Washington DC represented by the angry eagle head.

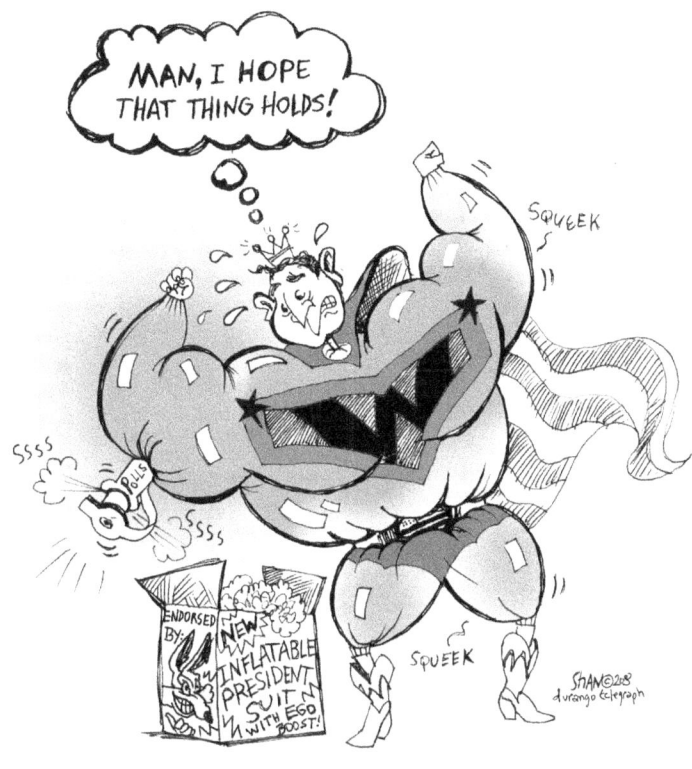

One of the great things about being in a movement is that you can believe what you want to believe...if you spend enough time listening to people asserting what you want to hear. It's also one of the worst things. Bush's polling ended at 63% for 2003, a historic high, so this cartoon is pure fantasy with no reality intruding.

After 2004, I stopped listening to alternative news sources like *Democracy Now* with such ardent regularity. I realized they were influencing my thought too much in one direction. This isn't to say that such media are not fabulous examples of free speech, disseminating information gained in no other way. However, like anything in life, there needs to be balance or too much time is spent in a world that simply does not exist.

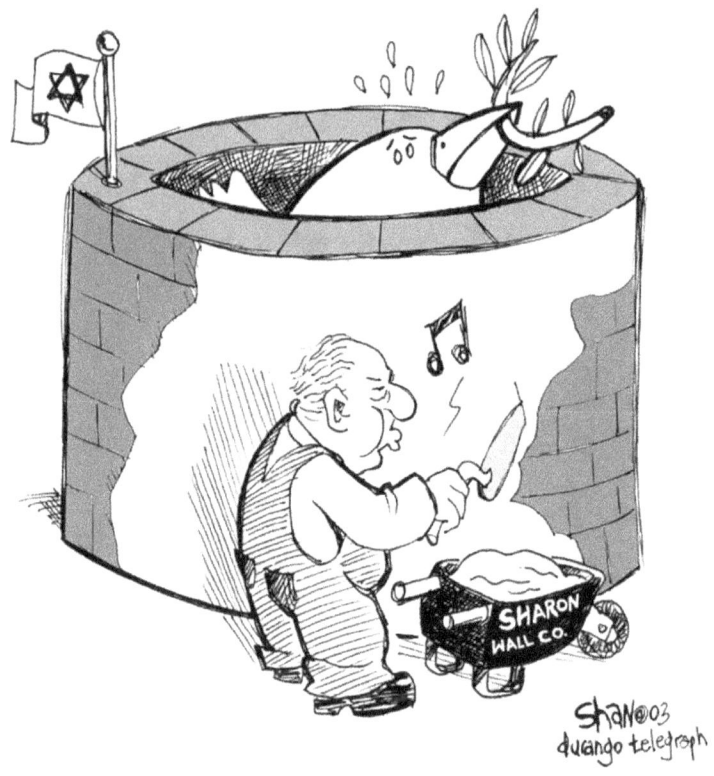

This cartoon is not the published version. Ariel Sharon's nose was twice as large in the original. Durango's local population of Jewish Nationalists busted me for that, and I deserved it. I had done exactly what they accused me of, creating a caricature that was right out of 1930's anti-Semitic propaganda.

I apologized privately and publicly for the offense, realizing that I would have to pay closer attention to my drawings if I was going to continue to cartoon. Although some public figures may indeed have outsized facial characteristics, a sensitivity to historic portrayals is essential. Why I didn't catch the big nose = bad Jew cue the first time around I can only chalk up to inattentiveness.

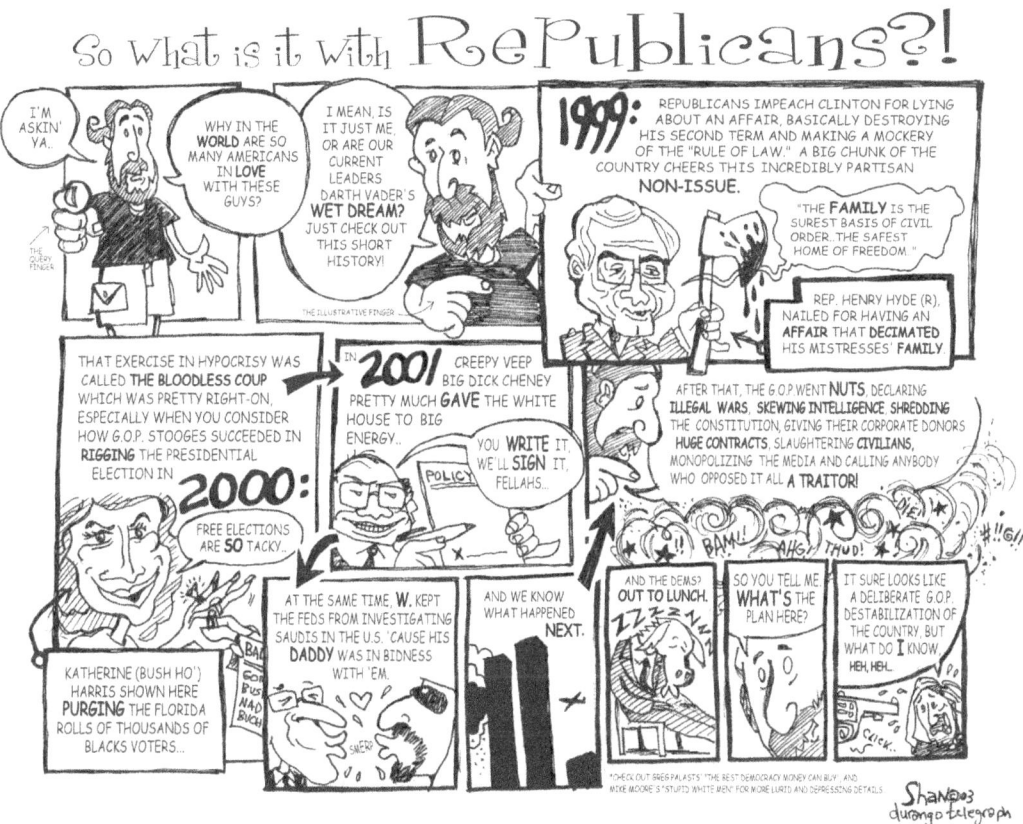

Joe Matt wrote an extremely interesting series of books called *Peepshow* that were basically a biography of his life. I was inspired to insert myself from time to time into my work as a narrator, or interrogator, much along the same lines.

This cartoon marked one of the few times I experimented with digital type, instead of hand-lettering. Although the legibility of the toon was good, the feel was artificial. It lacked the crunchy-ness of drawn letters that I've always loved.

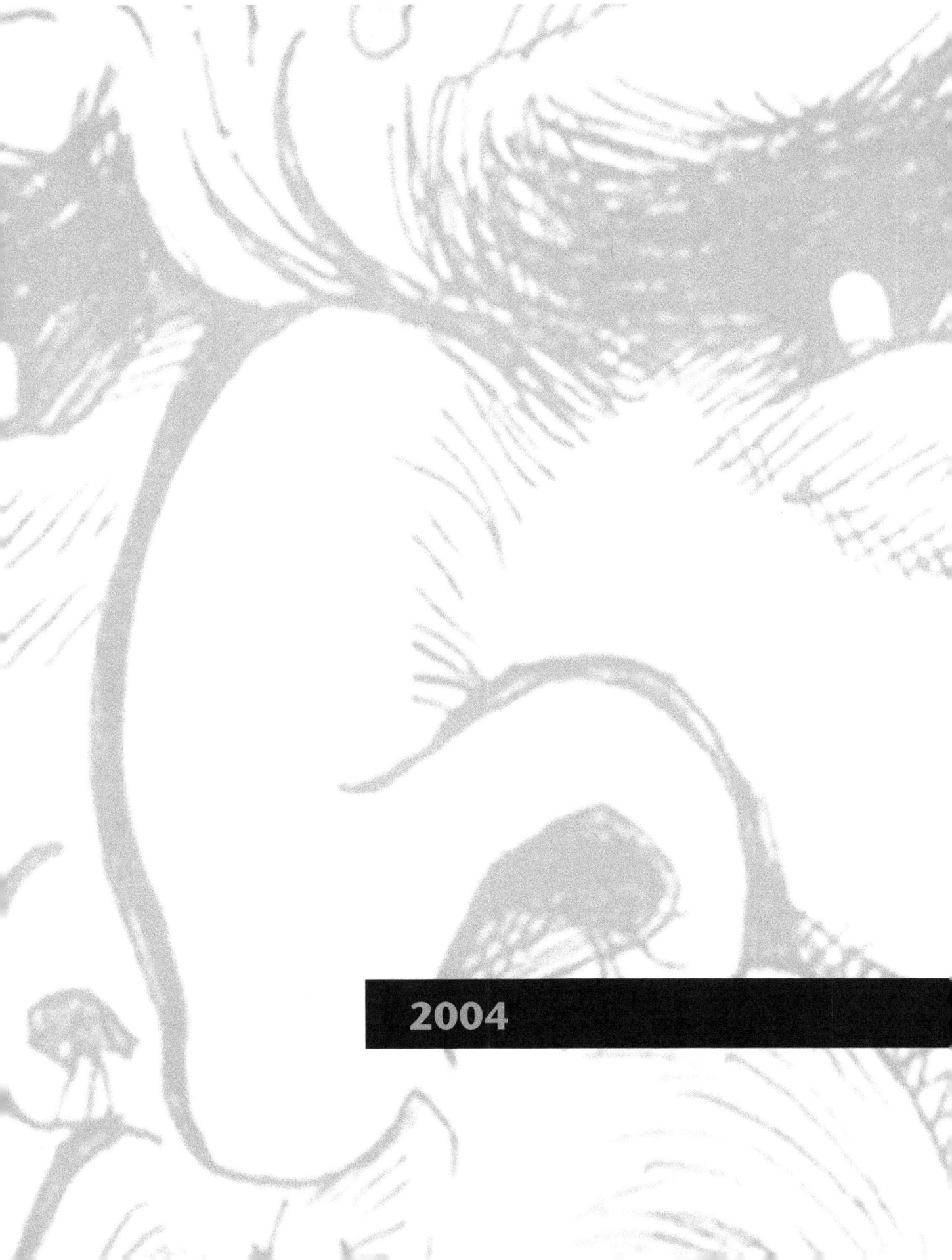

2004

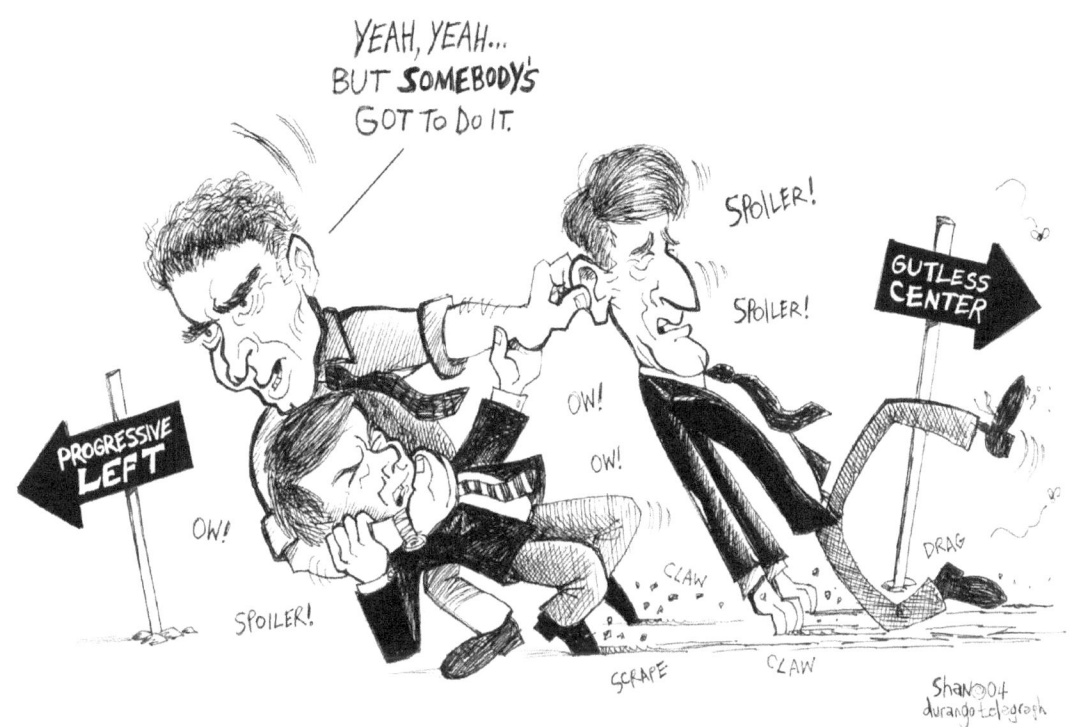

Ralph Nader famously split the progressive presidential vote in 2000 by running as a Green. I was a Green Party member at the time, and later went on to start a local chapter of the Green Party, along with seven other intrepid souls. We lasted 3 years before running out of steam.

This cartoon is a relic of an idealistic desire for pure progressive values to dominate the Democratic party, as well as that same idealism being subsumed by pragmatic understanding. Despite my intense longing for it, America will never be as Green as I had hoped. I joined the local Dems shortly thereafter and have been pushing a progressive agenda ever since.

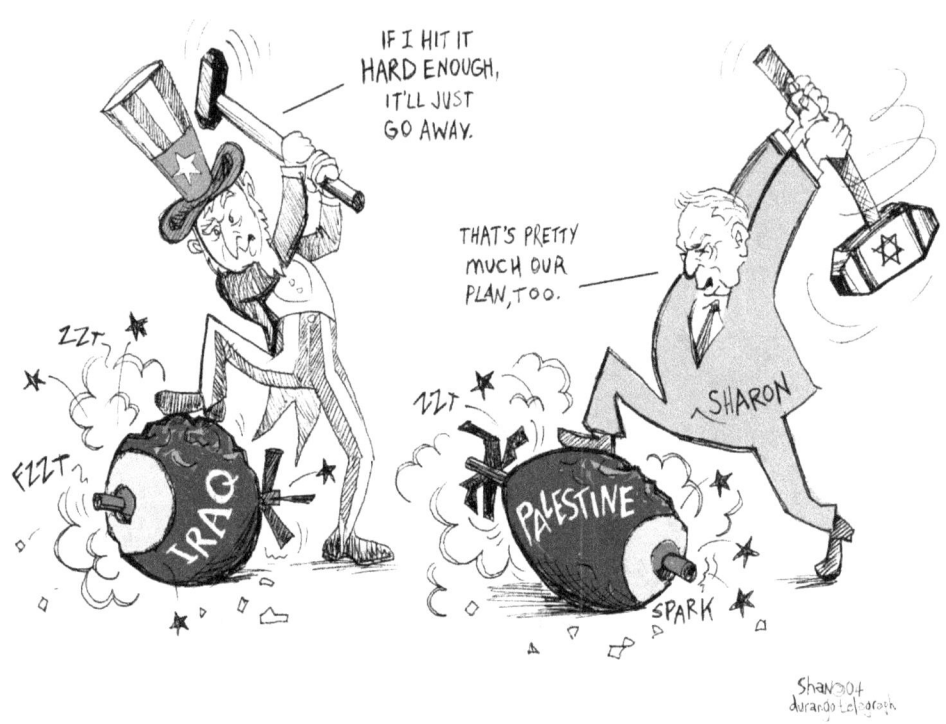

Around the time I made this cartoon, I was approached by a member of Durango's Jewish community, and we argued ourselves to a standstill about the history of the Israeli/Palestinian divide. He suggested we meet for dinner at the home of an Israeli couple that was spending the summer in Durango. I agreed, but stipulated that we would not talk politics, and could I bring my family? Of course, the answer was yes.

My memory of the dinner was delightful. The couple and their son were gracious hosts, and the fresh hummus was the best I'd ever eaten. Over the years, I've debated whether I should have engaged them. I doubt we would have made any headway, and doubted it at the time, which was why I made the stipulation of no shop talk. But I did walk away from that session with a sense of real people, engaged in what they see as a struggle for their lives. The session helped me to understand both sides more fully, and perhaps that was the idea all along.

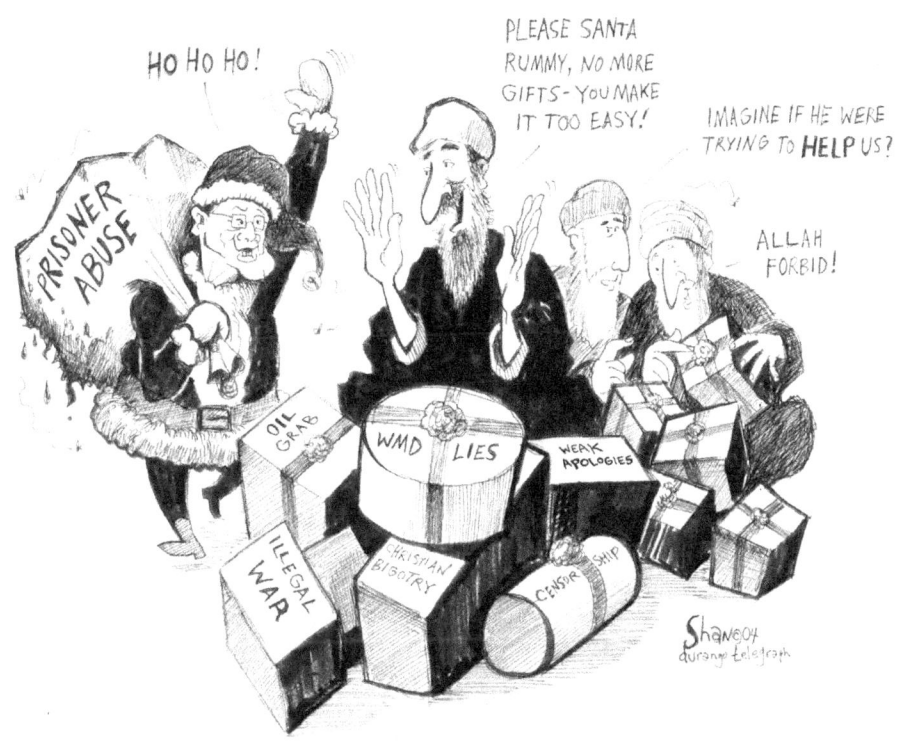

By 2004, the wheels were coming off the Iraq bus. It was quite clear that there were no WMD's, as Cheney, Powell, Rumsfeld and Rice had all promised us. Then Abu Graib burst like a diseased pimple, and the show got really dirty. It was no accident that an administration determined to use torture, seeing it as the only viable way to get information, would authorize sadistic, systematic abuse of prisoners in their power.

The image actually marks a turning point in my art, as I realized here that the use of black, just as R. Crumb said, makes a stronger, more graphically impacting image. My professors back at art school often said the same, but apparently, I needed to relearn it.

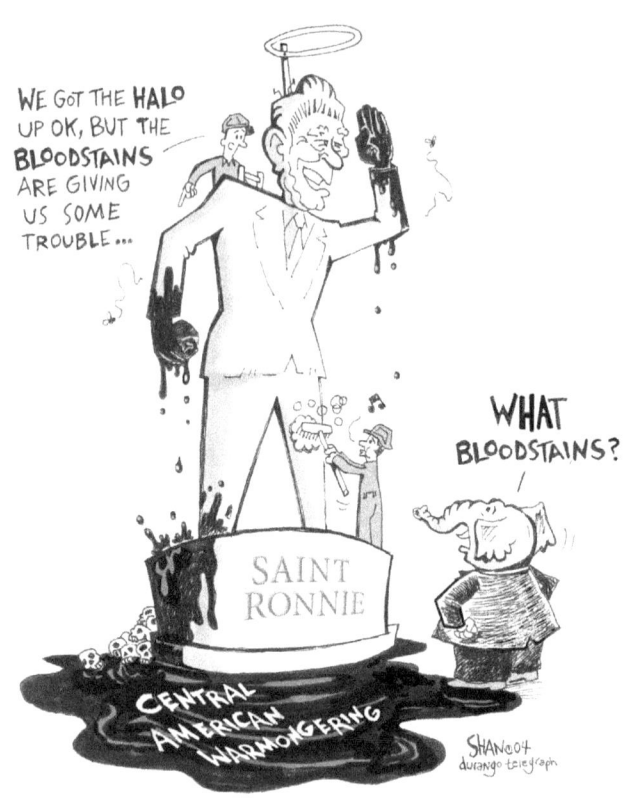

When Ronald Reagan died in 2004, there was a tremendous outpouring of grief from the right, most of which was of an entirely propagandized nature aimed at tying his legacy to Bush. There was also a lot of mainstream whitewash about who the man was.

I cut my political eyeteeth on Reagan, going from supporting his election because my parents had, to despising his policies because they were clearly anti-human. Anyone that could fail to understand trees are a necessary part of the biosphere, call ketchup a vegetable, and describe psychotic Central American terrorists as "the moral equivalent of our founding fathers," was not worth much.

Later on, I found out how Reagan struggled with and changed his views on nuclear war, after having been scared to death by the Able Archer incident in 1983, and embraced *rapprochement* with the Soviets. As ever, there is always some white in the black.

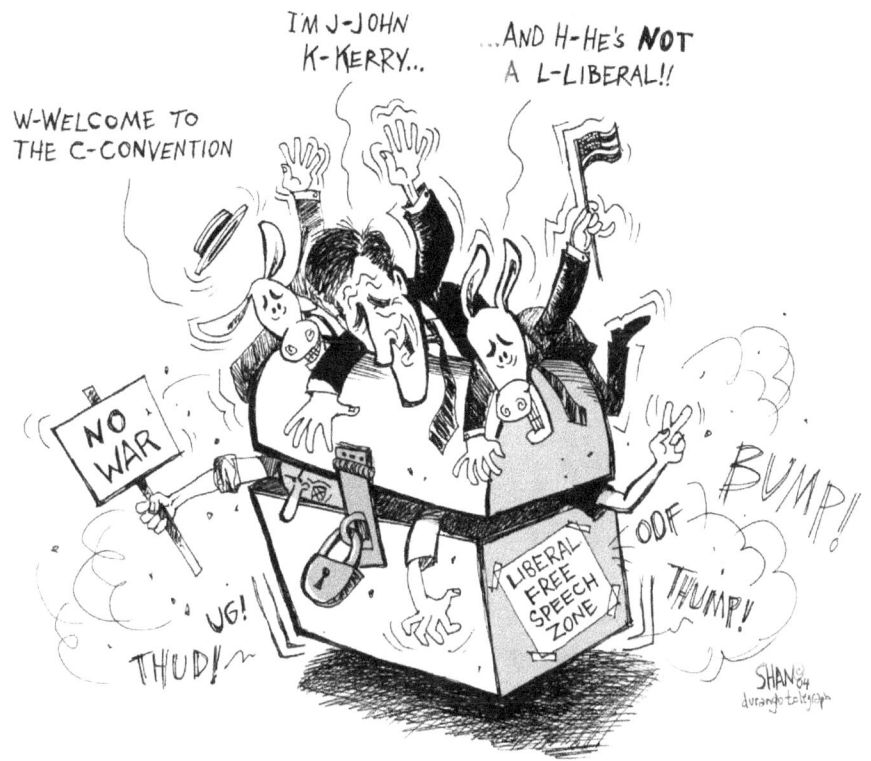

I wanted Howard Dean as the Democratic Nominee in 2004, and was surprised that Kerry ran away with it after an initial poor showing. Things got even weirder as the Democrats decided to run on a, "we're more patriotic bad-asses than you," platform, which of course, didn't work. What was even more depressing was the censorship of the anti-war left chunk of the party at the 2004 convention.

I've never understood why progressives run away from our history. We have so much to be proud of. Someday, maybe we'll get a candidate that actually feels the same way.

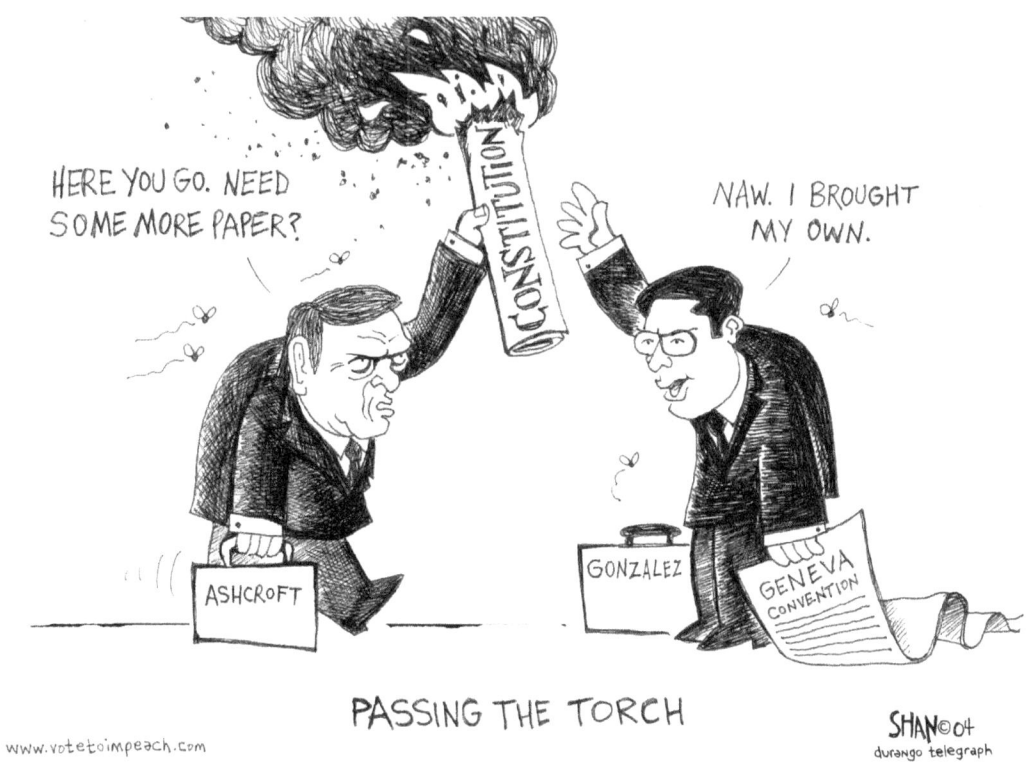

PASSING THE TORCH

SHAN©04
durango telegraph

I have to say, I thought it was not possible to have a worse Attorney General than John Ashcroft. G.W. managed to find one though. Ashcroft, although a horrendous Neanderthal, was at least cognizant of the law enough to refuse to reauthorize the illegal warrantless surveillance program initiated during the first Bush term, something Alberto Gonzalez had no problem with.

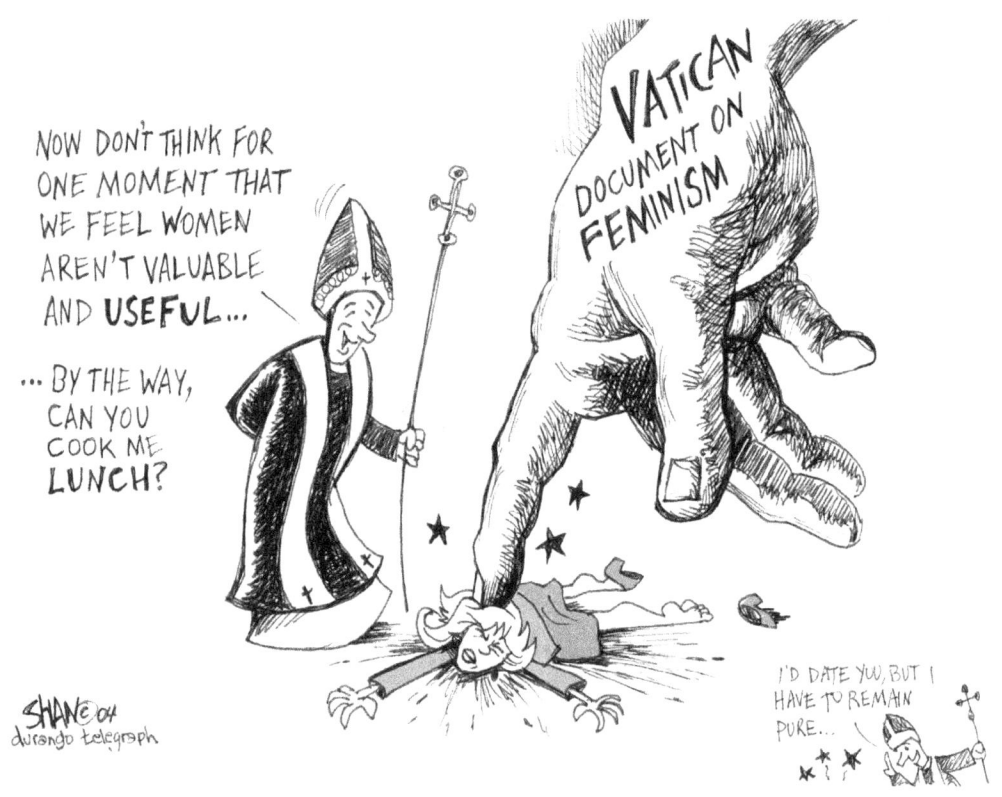

The 2004 Vatican Letter on Feminism decried the "distortions" and "lethal effects" of feminism, which it defined as an effort to blur the differences between men and women. The statement said such activity undermines the "natural two-parent structure" of the family and makes "homosexuality and heterosexuality virtually equivalent."

Of course, definitions and judgements on women's issues from a group of celibate octogenarians worried about their power base are always illuminating.

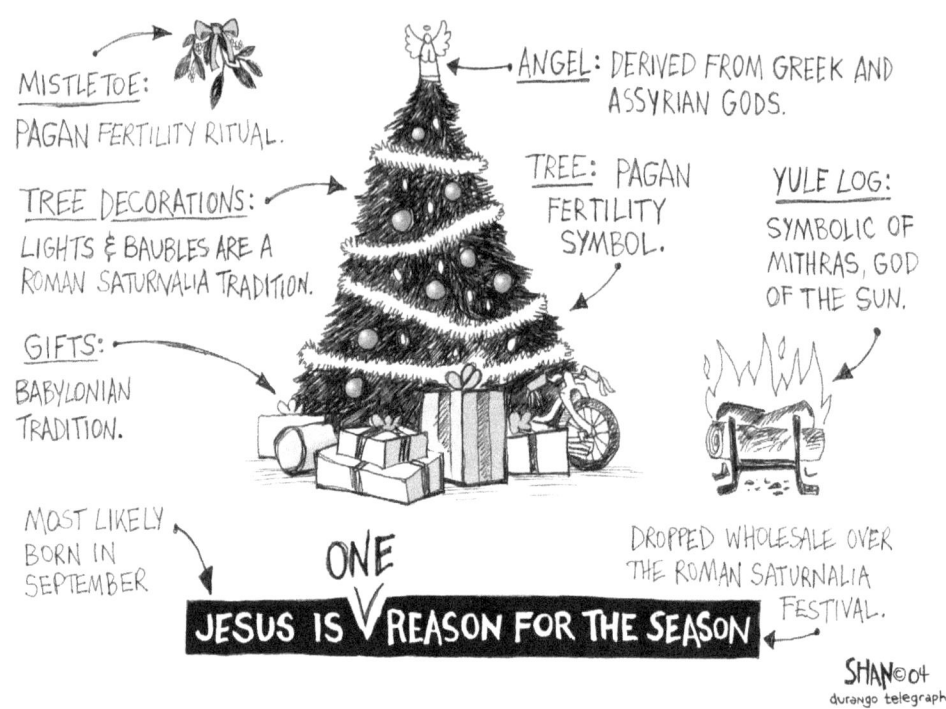

MISTLETOE:
PAGAN FERTILITY RITUAL.

ANGEL: DERIVED FROM GREEK AND ASSYRIAN GODS.

TREE DECORATIONS:
LIGHTS & BAUBLES ARE A ROMAN SATURNALIA TRADITION.

TREE: PAGAN FERTILITY SYMBOL.

YULE LOG:
SYMBOLIC OF MITHRAS, GOD OF THE SUN.

GIFTS:
BABYLONIAN TRADITION.

MOST LIKELY BORN IN SEPTEMBER

ONE
JESUS IS ⋁ REASON FOR THE SEASON

DROPPED WHOLESALE OVER THE ROMAN SATURNALIA FESTIVAL.

SHAN©04
durango telegraph

I don't have any problem with Christian pride in Christmas, and the devotional activities surrounding their interpretation of the holiday. Christmas is big enough for all of us. What does rile me, however, is the consistent insistence that the holiday belongs to Christians alone.

As this cartoon shows, that is plainly not the case.

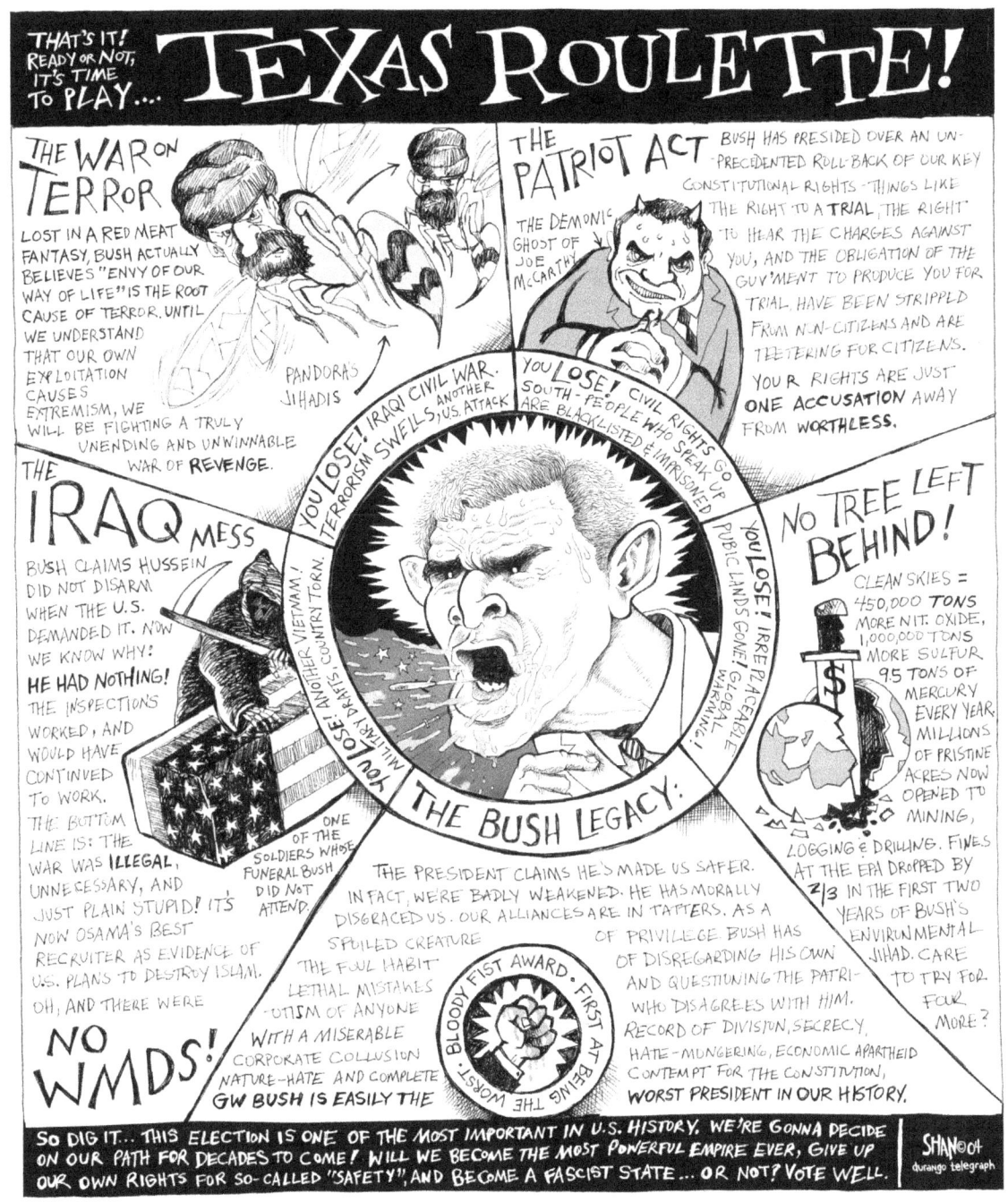

I, like most progressives, was completely astonished that America could possibly give G.W. another term. This work was a full page, fire-breathing attempt to deny what seemed all too likely on the eve of the election: a Bush victory. Like 2000, the 2004 contest ended, initially, with a draw that lengthened into the next day, when Kerry conceded, refusing to dispute Bush's dubious win in Ohio.

The breathless, hysterical tone of this cartoon reflects the way the left felt at time-desperate to make the rest of the country see what a mess Bush had made. Unfortunately, we failed.

2005

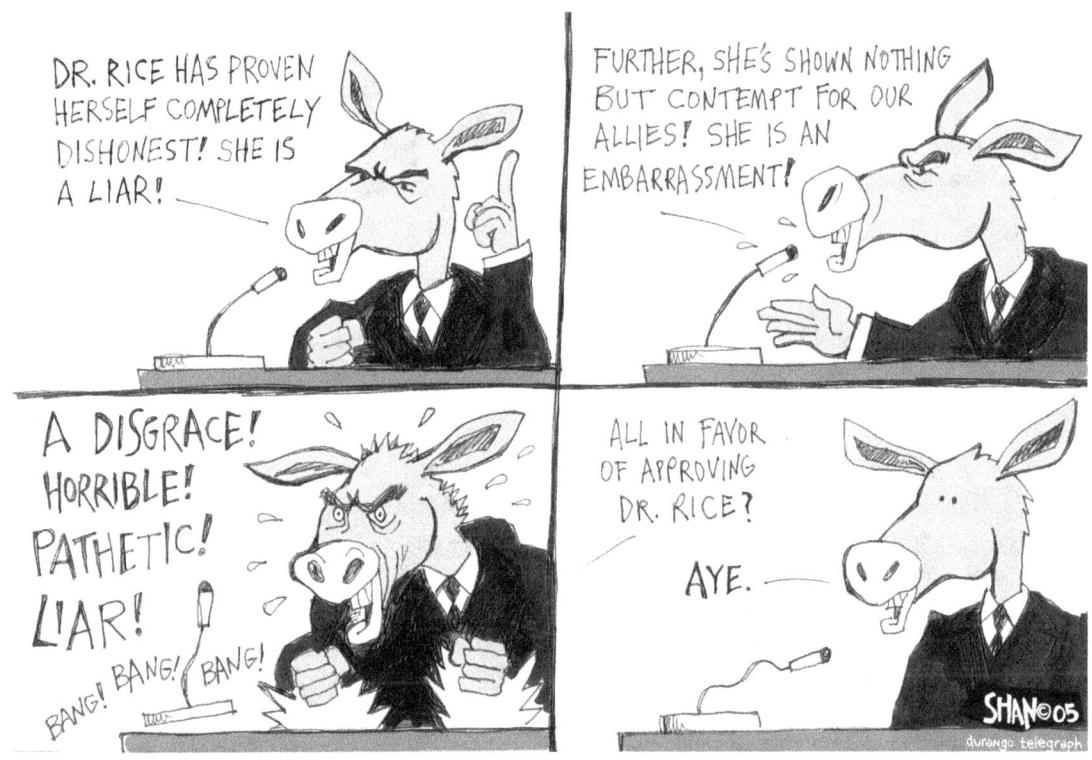

In so many ways, this cartoon sums up the way Democrats were perceived during the Bush years. Outraged, yet compliant. While democracy is by far the best system we've yet developed for governing our frail humanity, it is far from perfect. Any system that allows such a capitulation to personal advancement is seriously flawed.

Making works that criticize the folks that you voted for is hard. Yet becoming politically mature requires that you see the machinations of power for what they are, and understand the practicality of governance.

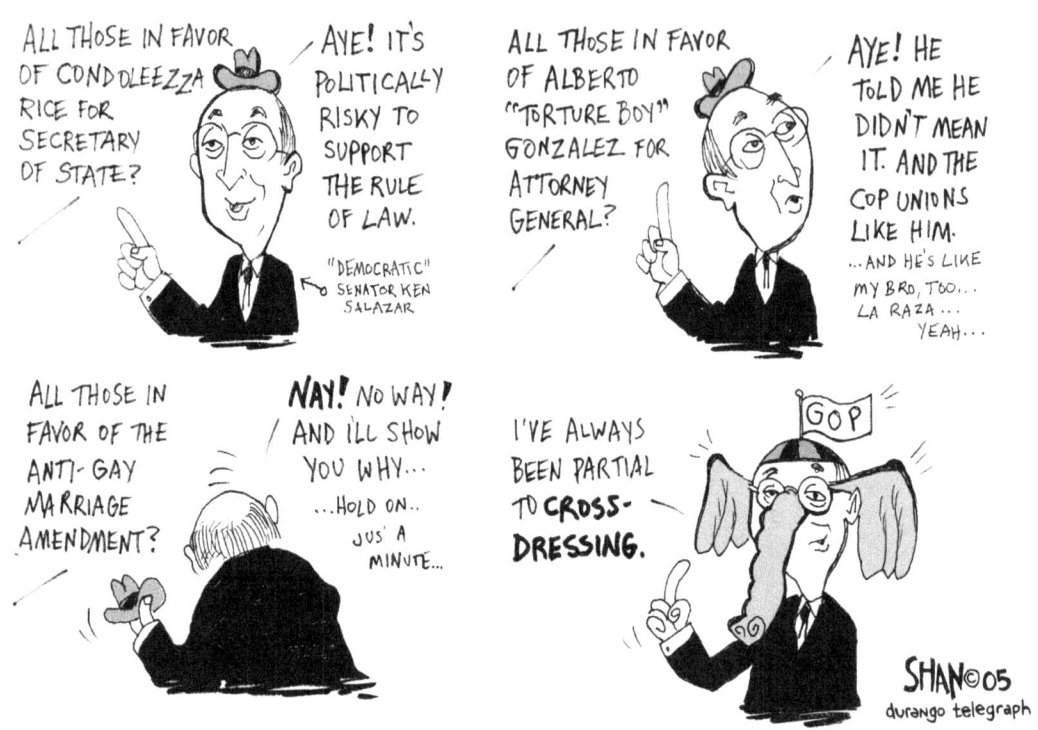

Previous to becoming Secretary of the Interior, Ken Salazar was my senator. We had a tempestuous relationship. I'd yell at the TV when he did something I didn't like, and he'd keep right on doing it. This is how a blue dog and his liberal constituency relate. It's a tough gig, seeing as how replacing Ken with some conservative fellow only too happy to slice and dice the land was less appealing than keeping Ken and putting up with his foibles. And, in all fairness, he's done some really good stuff.

As it was, this toon cost me some grief with the more practical Democratic staffers.

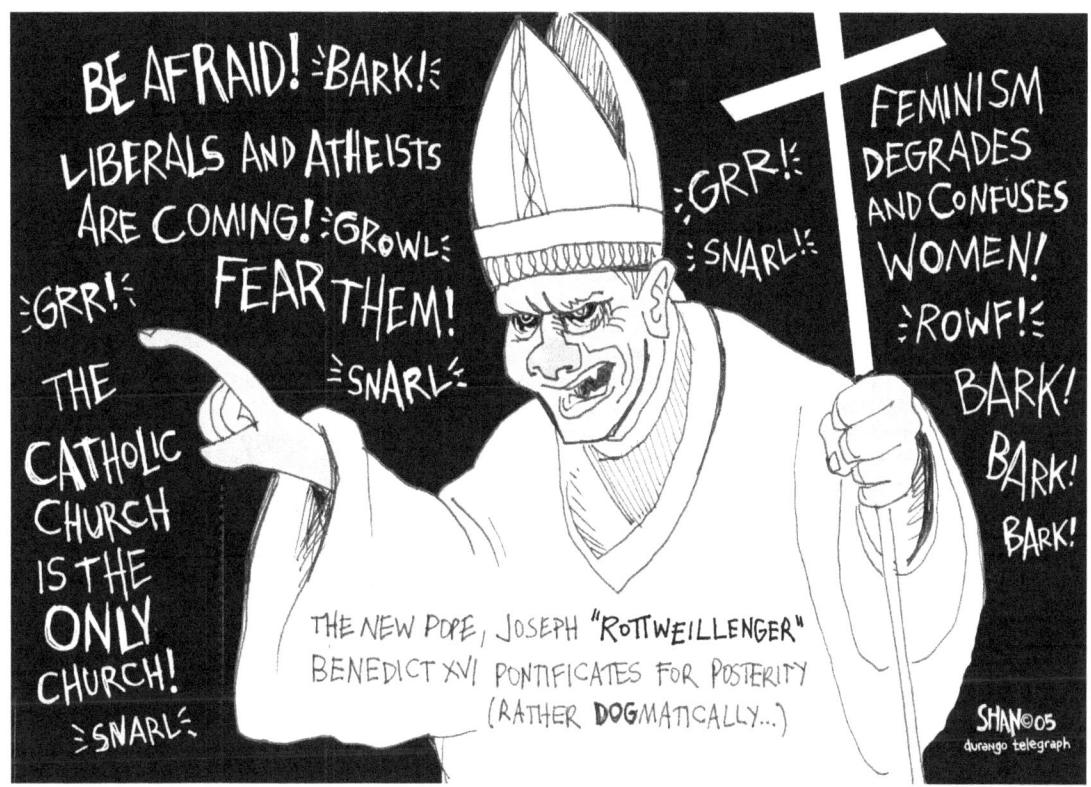

Pope John Paul II died in the spring of 2005, and it's interesting to note that the Catholic School where I celebrate St. Patrick's day every year still hasn't taken down his photo and replaced it with the current Pope, Benedict XVI. Where John Paul seemed authentically concerned for the poor and dedicated to a great dialog with other religions, Benedict seems intent on pissing people off. He certainly got off to a good start doing that with his ascension to the high office, making several remarks about feminism in particular that were vintage 1850.

While I regularly get hate mail about my treatment of Israel, this particular cartoon caused an up-roar in the Catholic quarters. Strangely, all I was doing was essentially repeating back the amazing nonsense the new Pope was freely spouting.

ALICIA WHITE, 15   THURLENE STILLDAY, 15   CHANELLE ROSEBEAR, 15
CHASE LUSSIER, 15   DEWAYNE LEWIS, 15   DARYL LUSSIER, 58
MICHELLE SIGANA, 32   DERRICK BRUN, 28   NEVA ROGERS, 62

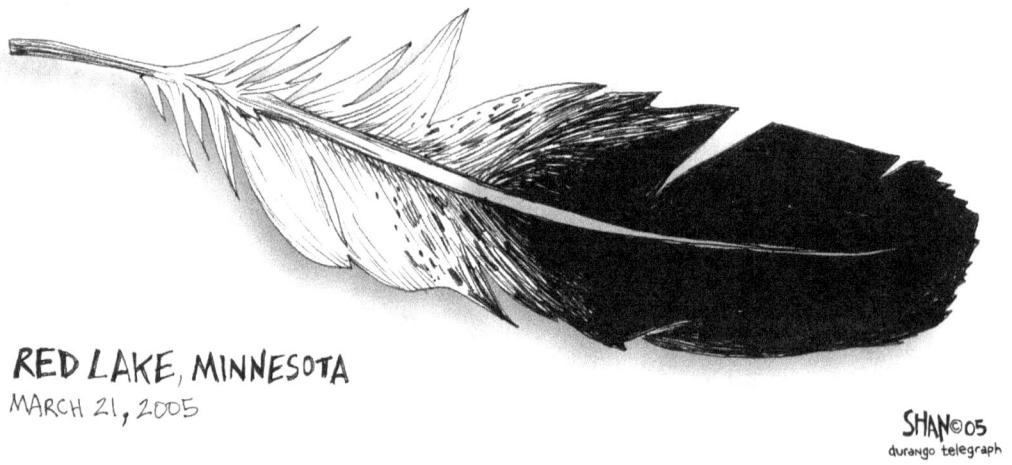

RED LAKE, MINNESOTA
MARCH 21, 2005

SHAN©05
durango telegraph

Coming fairly soon after the Columbine shootings in Colorado, the Red Lake massacre in Minnesota made national headlines, but was not subject to the endless dissection which seemed to permeate our media for years after the former tragedy. No one made a movie about it, no one yelled at the NRA for having a gun show in Minnesota after it. The event faded quickly from national consciousness, and the only reason I can think of is that the damage was done on a reservation to native children, rather than in a metropolitan suburb to white kids.

The feather, a symbol of power and spirituality in native cultures, is shown here as fallen, perhaps bloodstained.

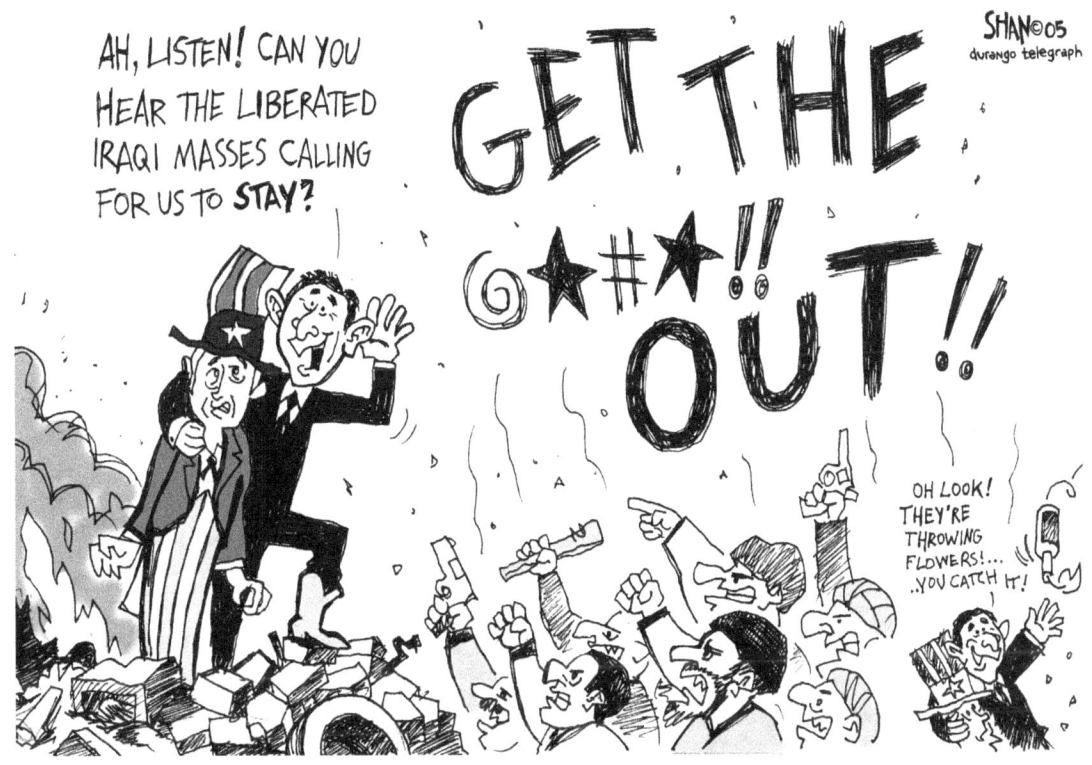

By 2005 it was becoming very clear that US forces in Iraq were not only failing to stem the rising tide of civic violence, but were in fact, causing a lot of the unrest simply by their presence there. US involvement in a complex political and cultural stew within the country caused them to become lighting rods for the shame and hatred Iraqis had of being occupied. The more our army tried to separate the two warring sides, the more we became the symbol of oppression.

Shi'a Iraqis began purging their neighborhoods of Sunnis, and the Sunnis did likewise. By 2007, entire sections of the country were segregated into religious go, no-go zones. Hundreds of thousands died in the aftermath, as long simmering anger over historical wounds spilled into a civil war.

By January , 2005, the hunt for non-existent "weapons of mass destruction," the entire justification for the US invasion, was declared over. None were ever found. Throughout it all, Bush remained publicly unconcerned, even making a joke in 2004 at a reporter's dinner about the "missing wmd."

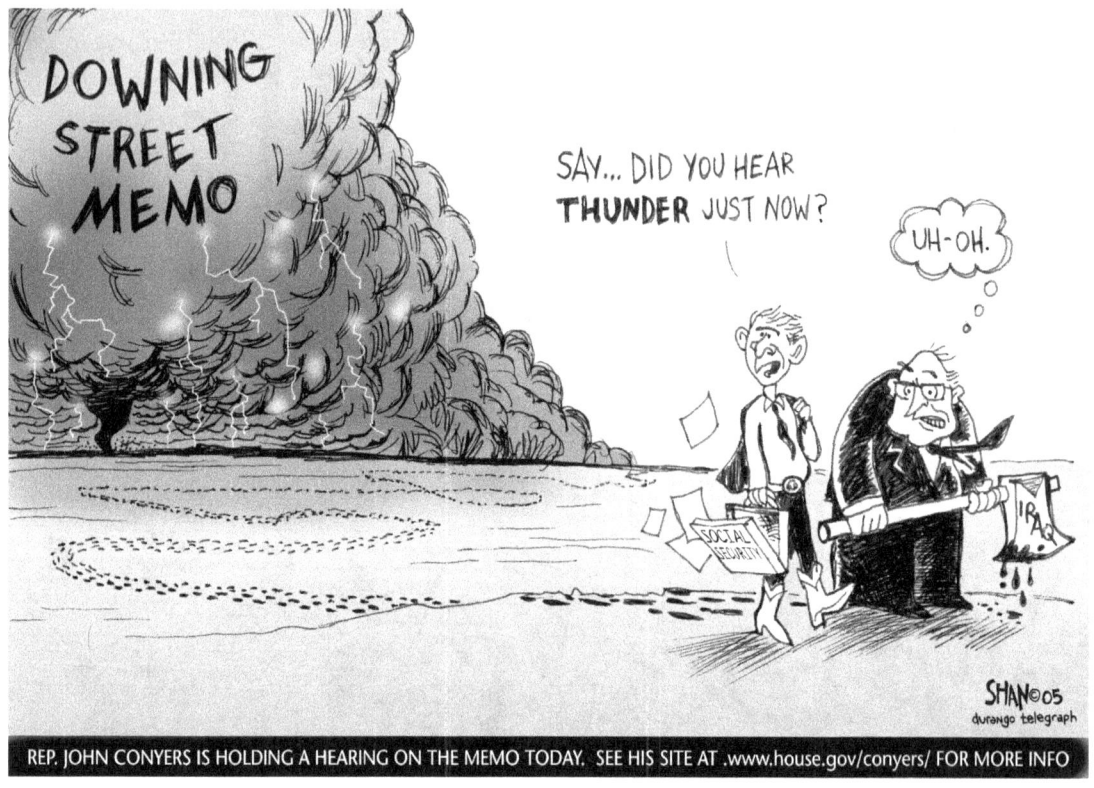

REP. JOHN CONYERS IS HOLDING A HEARING ON THE MEMO TODAY. SEE HIS SITE AT .www.house.gov/conyers/ FOR MORE INFO

In May of 2005, news the "Downing Street Memo" came crashing over the media like a tidal wave. The document was a leaked 2002 secret memo between the top British defense and intelligence officials, and it revealed that the US Administration was determined to invade Iraq to remove Saddam Hussein, using WMD as justification. The memo stated that intelligence and facts were being "fixed around this policy."

To those of us in the anti-war camp, this seemed to be the smoking gun we were looking for. It showed conclusively that Bush's rational for invasion was paper thin, and that lies were being concocted to whip up enough fear for war. However, it was not to be. While the authenticity of the document was never disputed, Congressional Democrats did not exploit the issue, perhaps because they also had voted to invade Iraq.

Whatever the reasons, the memo, while undercutting confidence in the Bush Administration, was not the impeachment bomb it had appeared at first blush.

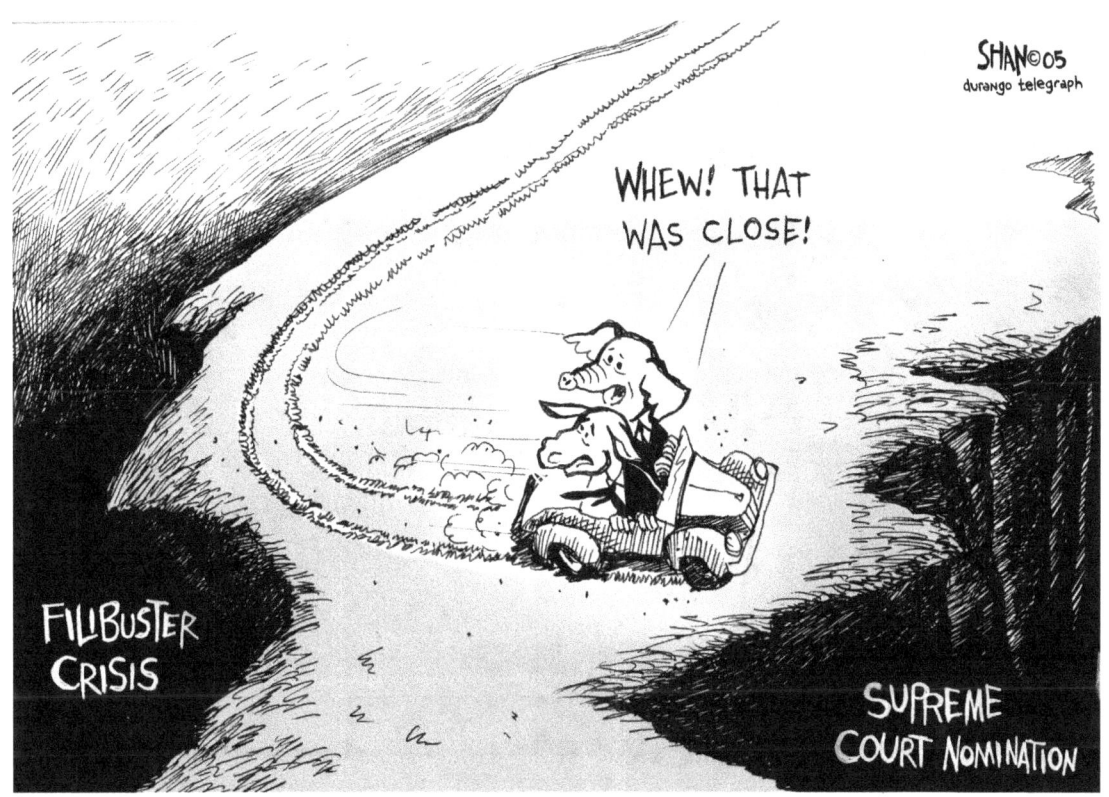

While the Democrats may have been cowed by their vote on war, by 2005 they had had enough of the Bush lemonade to start dumping it on the floor. By filibustering Bush's appellate court appointees, the Dems provoked a crisis. Republicans threatened to change Senate rules to eliminate the use of the filibuster to prevent judicial confirmation votes. This was called the "nuclear option." In response, the Dems threatened to shut the Senate down.

The stalemate was broken by the "Gang of 14," a bipartisan group of Senators that came up with a compromise which allowed five of the seven filibustered appointees to take the bench.

However, as so often is the case in politics, no sooner had once crisis finished, than another popped up, as bickering over the appointment of Supreme Court Justice John Roberts drove the Senate into an uproar again.

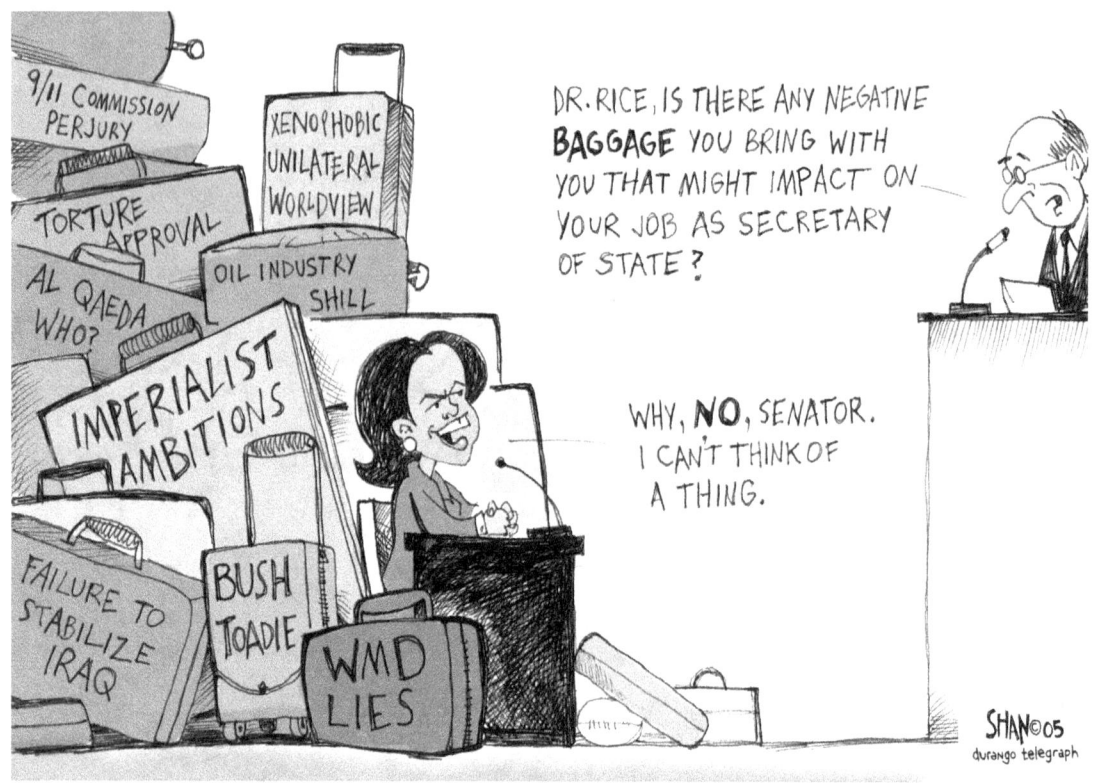

With the re-election of Bush in 2004 came the departure of many top officials in the administration. Colin Powell, the hapless Secretary of State who had come before the UN in 2003 to plead a lie about yellow cake uranium, stepped down, and Condoleeza Rice, Bush's former National Security Adviser took up the job.

As this was the woman who had ignored the outgoing Clinton Administration's painfully specific warnings about Osama Bin Laden's plans to strike the US with planes...and as she was the cheerleader behind invading Iraq, even using the term "mushroom cloud" when describing the possible effects of not doing so, her appointment to the top diplomatic spot was seen by the left as yet another cynical corruption of a department that was meant to defuse global tensions, not escalate them.

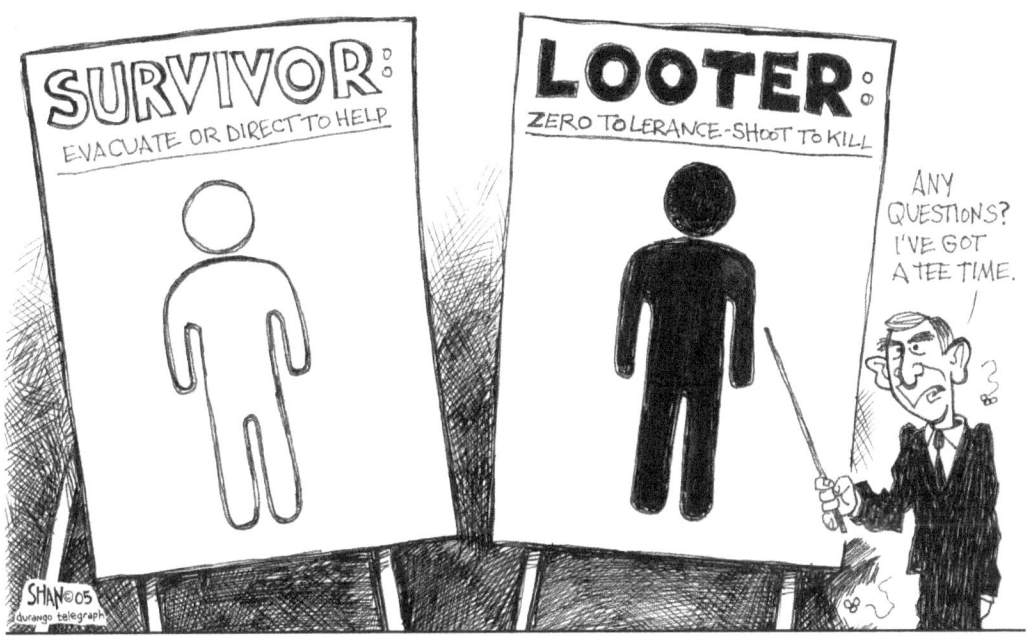

Hurricane Katrina slammed into New Orleans in 2005, inflicting $90.3 billion dollars worth of damage and killing 1,836 Americans. Stories about selective law enforcement of and assistance to the city's black residents emerged almost immediately.

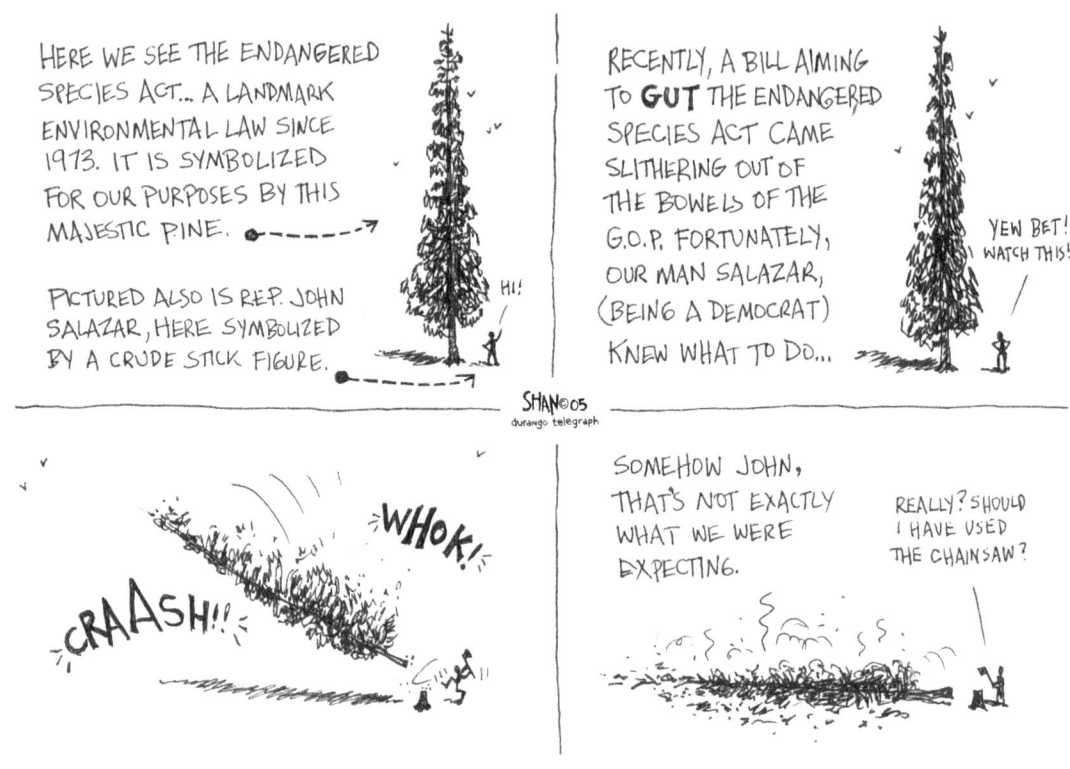

While John Salazar certainly moved to the left as the Obama Administration ramped up, his roots as a property rights advocate were never far from the surface during the Bush years.

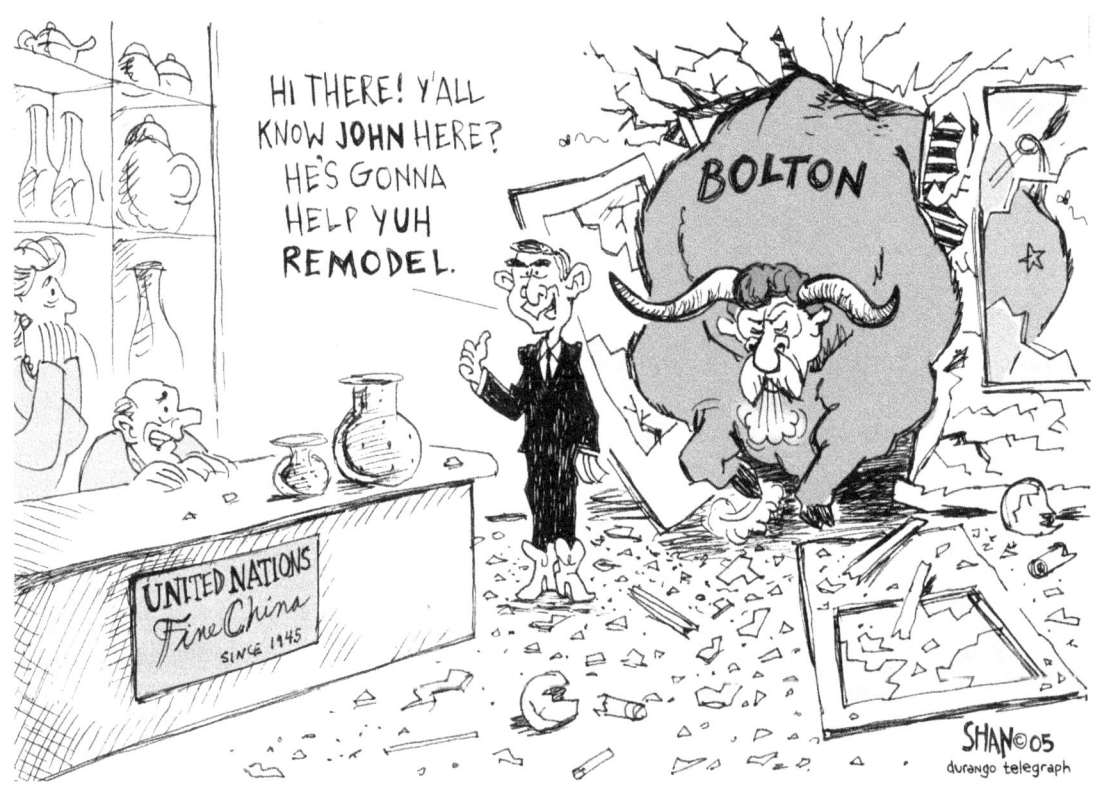

In 1994, John Bolton stated:

> "There is no such thing as the United Nations. There is only the international community, which can only be led by the only remaining superpower, which is the United States."

In 2005, G.W. Bush recess-appointed Bolton US Ambassador to the U.N. Much like Condi Rice's appointment, most of America could only view this act as one of complete hostility towards the idea of getting along with the rest of the world.

Little wonder then, that the Nobel Committee gave President Obama the Peace Prize in 2009 simply for reversing such boneheaded maneuvers.

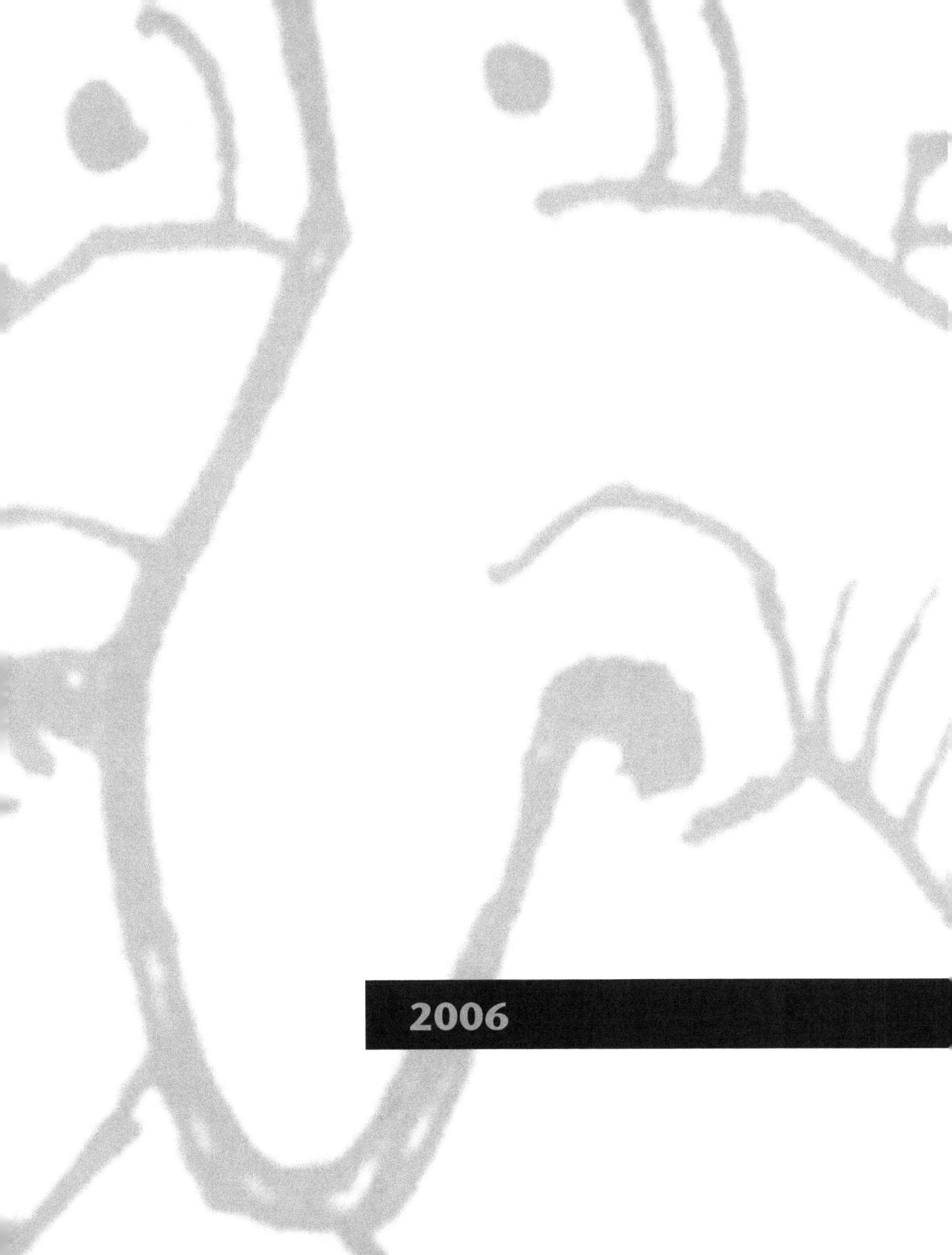

2006

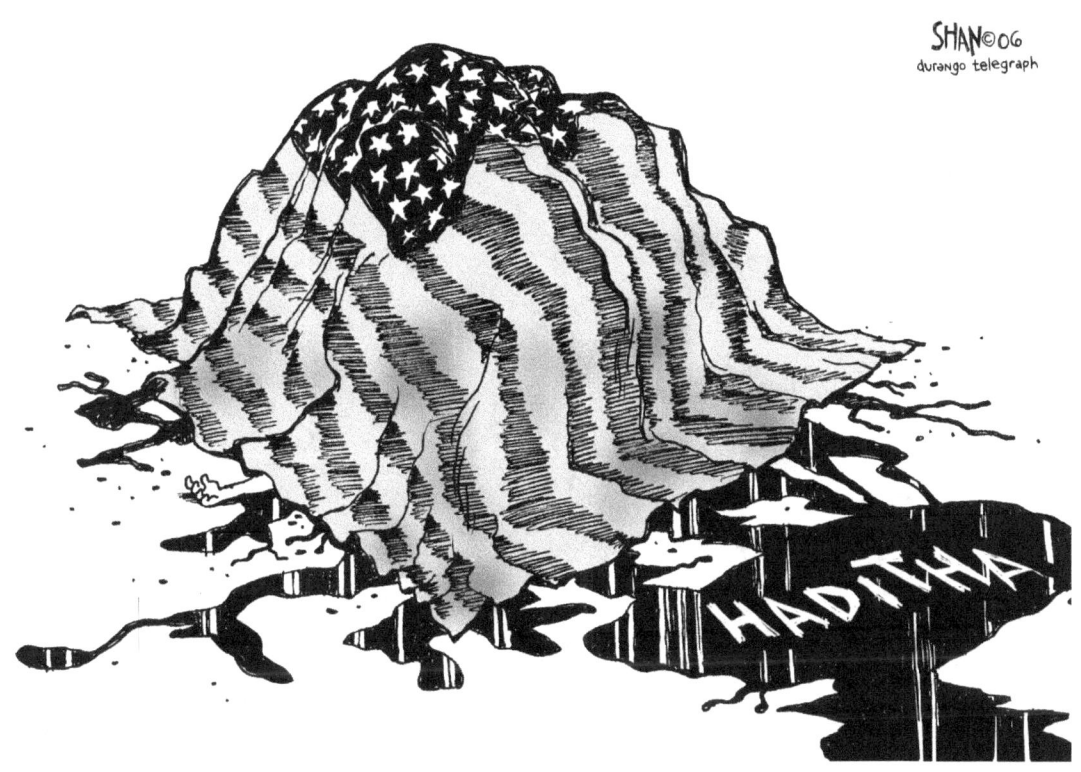

On November 19, 2005, 24 men, women, and children were brutally massacred in Haditha, Iraq by US forces. At least 15 were noncombatants. One victim was a year old baby girl. The killings were alleged retribution for an IED attack on a convoy of Marines. The cover-up began almost immediately thereafter, and no investigation was instigated until a 2006 *Time* story.

As of 2010, no American soldier had been convicted of the crime.

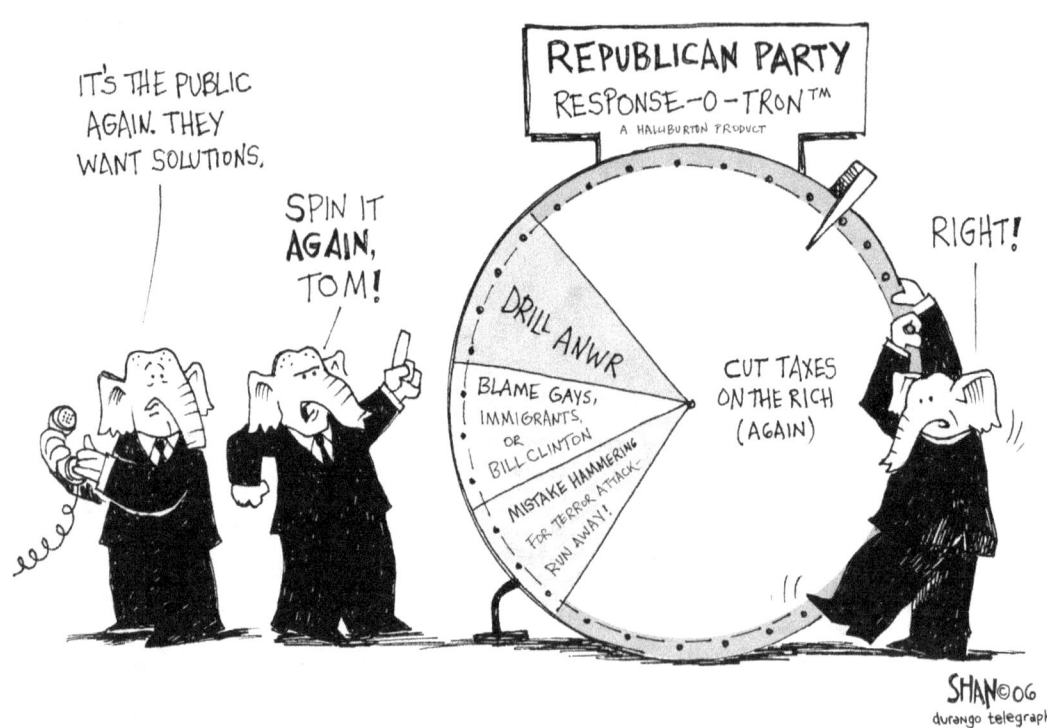

By 2006, Congressional Republicans were deep in the weeds. Restricted by a free-market ideology that allowed only tax cuts as a legitimate solution to every economic problem, their refusal to compromise foreshadowed their drubbing in the 2006 midterms.

WOMAN & CHILD KILLED BY
TERRORISTS

WOMAN & CHILD KILLED BY
THE ADVANCE OF DEMOCRACY

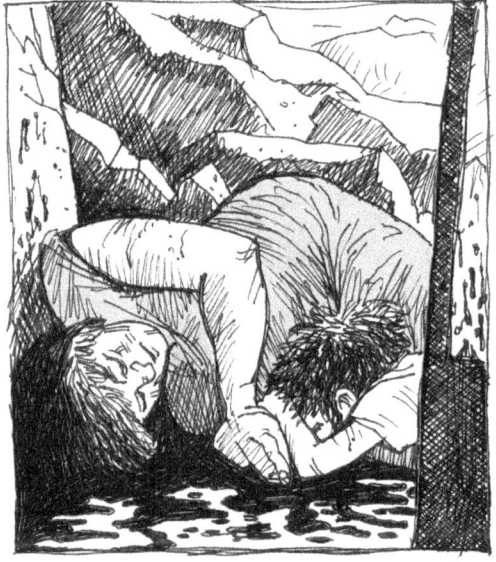 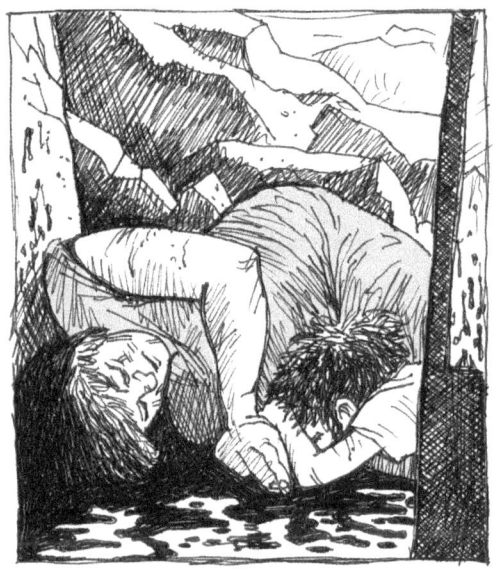

SHAN©06
durango telegraph

Israel's 2006 assault on Lebanon killed 1,300 Lebanese, and displaced around 1 million. Israel justified the attack as a response to rockets sent over the border by Hezbollah militants. The conflict raged for 34 days, leaving large parts of Lebanon destroyed and the militia shattered.

Such an abandonment of the peace process by the Bush Administration, and in fact, it's actual cheerleading of this conflict, reveals a cynicism of the darkest kind.

My cartoon was an attempt to show that death is death, and it is always ugly, no matter the reasons or rationalizations put forward. The drawing was taken from a real photograph of a mother and her baby killed in the assault.

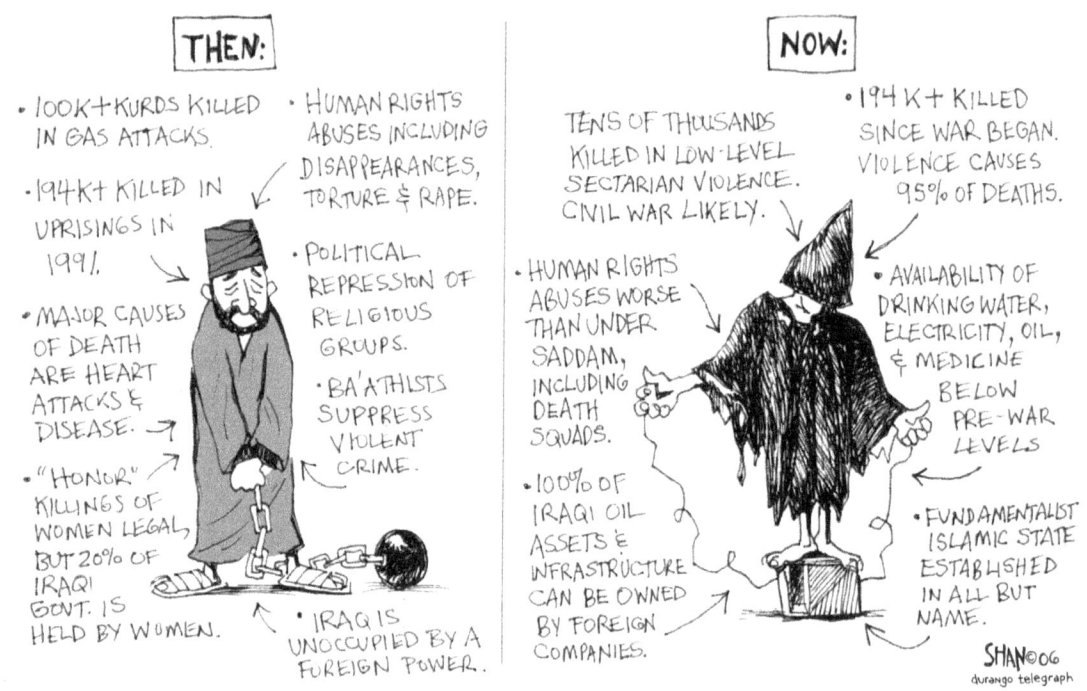

While the Iraq war was not justified in any way, and was in fact, based on a lie, the Iraqi people were hardly enjoying a free, democratic government when ruled by Saddam Hussein. This work addressed the ludicrous assertion that humanity's problems are black and white, composed of evil doers and good guys. Reality is complex and difficult, but the end result of an elective, illegal war for profit is always going to be bad.

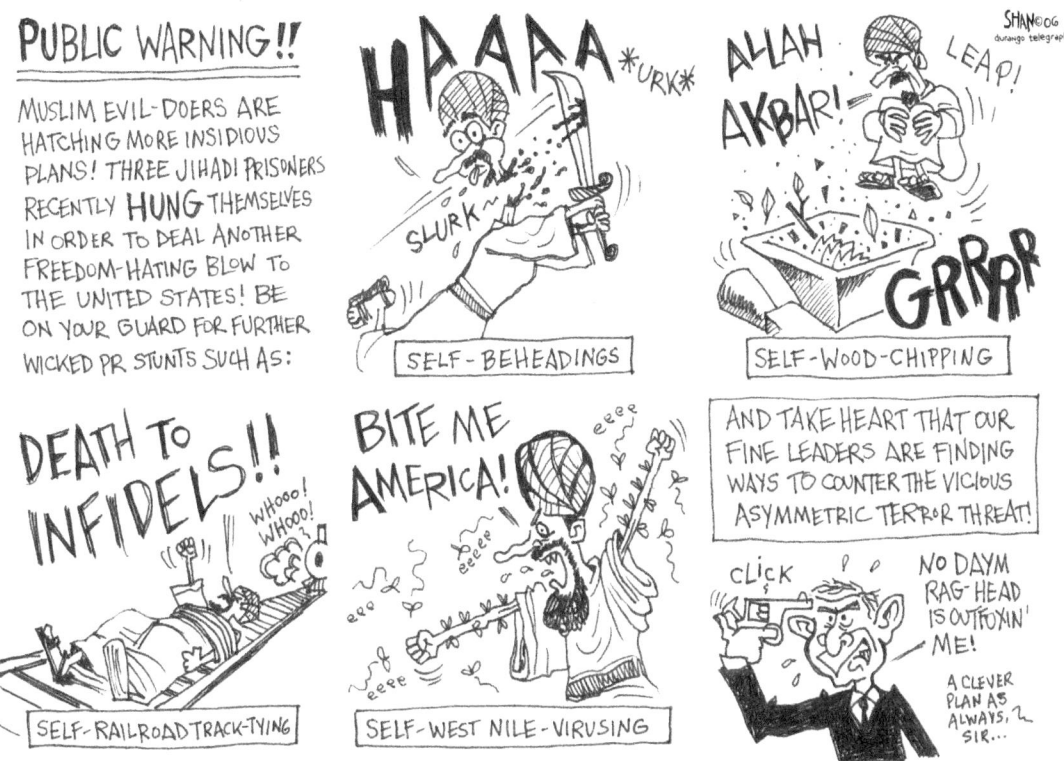

Three prisoners held at Guantanamo Bay in Cuba by the US hanged themselves in what appeared to be an act of desperation to escape their harsh treatment, which included torture. Or at least, that's what the rational people listening to the story thought. The Guantanamo commander, Navy Rear Admiral Harry Harris, said that the men were committed Jihadists who committed an act of "asymmetric warfare... a tactic used by al-Qaida to garner support." I just rolled with that logic.

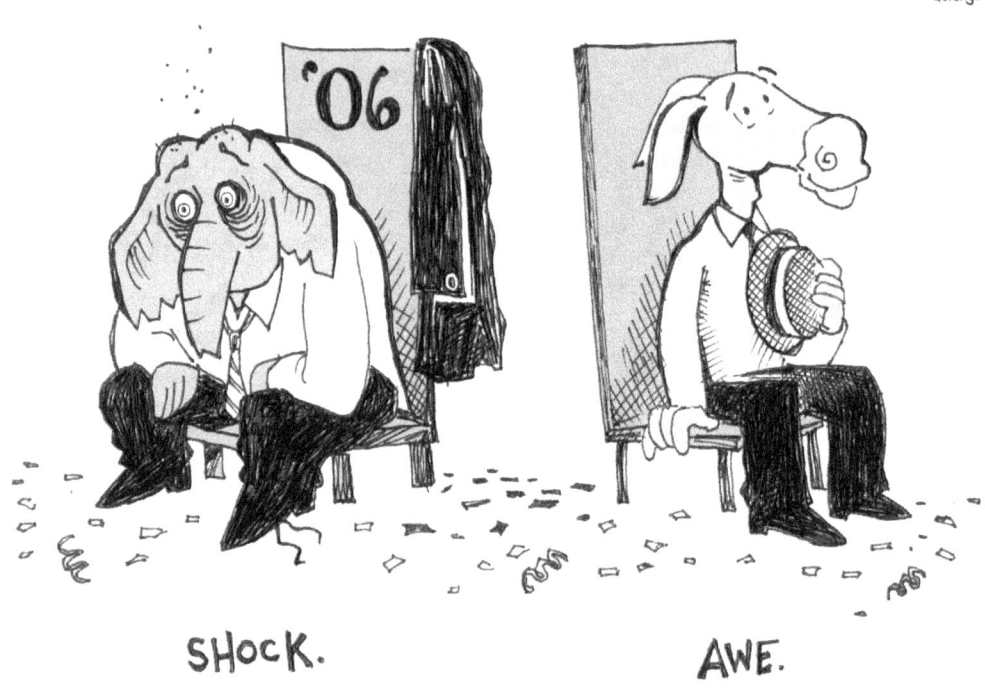

SHAN©06
durango telegraph

SHOCK.   AWE.

The 2006 midterm elections were described by President Bush as a "thumpin." He was right. Americans, sickened by years of war, incompetence and lies, voted a Democratic landslide. The Senate, House, the majority of Governorships, and many state legislatures were turned over to Dem control, leaving the GOP profoundly nonplussed, but stubbornly unapologetic.

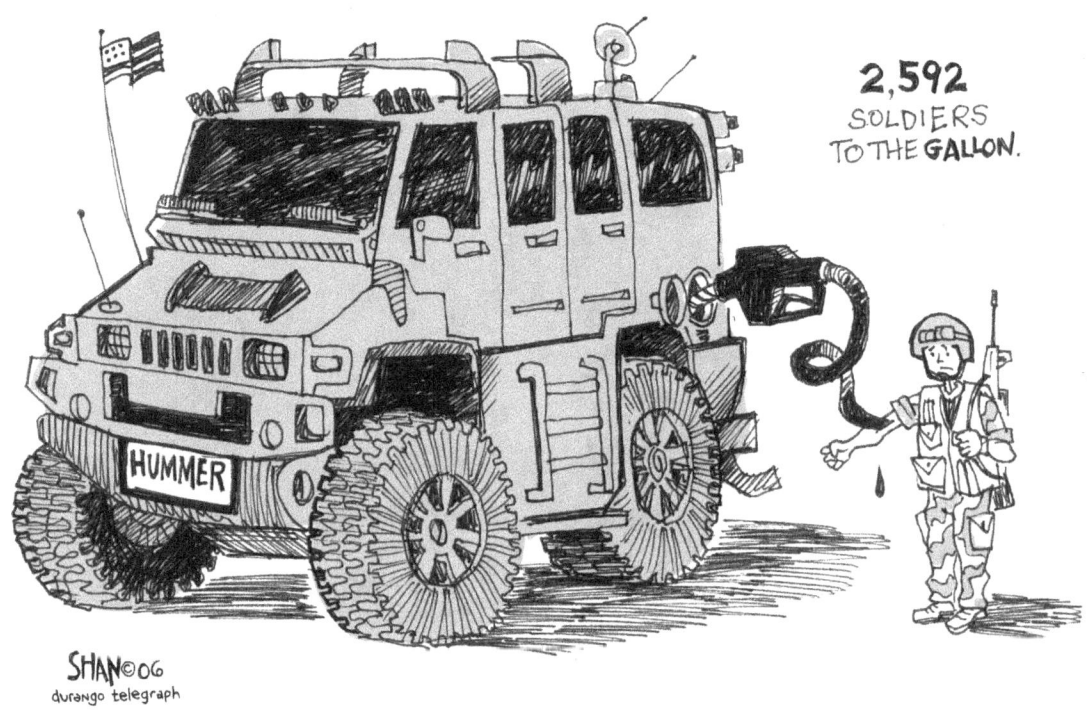

2,592
SOLDIERS
TO THE **GALLON**.

HUMMER

SHAN©06
durango telegraph

I've always hated the civilian version of the "hummer', or military HumVee, short for High Mobility Multipurpose Wheeled Vehicle. While the original vehicle looks sleek and responsive, the civilian version is a pig of car, averaging around 14 mpg. This fact, combined with it's outrageously expensive price tag, made it a target of anti-war and environmental activists during the 2010's.

My point was that Iraq, being primarily a colonial war of conquest to secure fossil fuel access, was driven by the insatiable desire of Americans to drive ridiculously huge SUVs. Thankfully, the entire line folded with the collapse of GM in 2009.

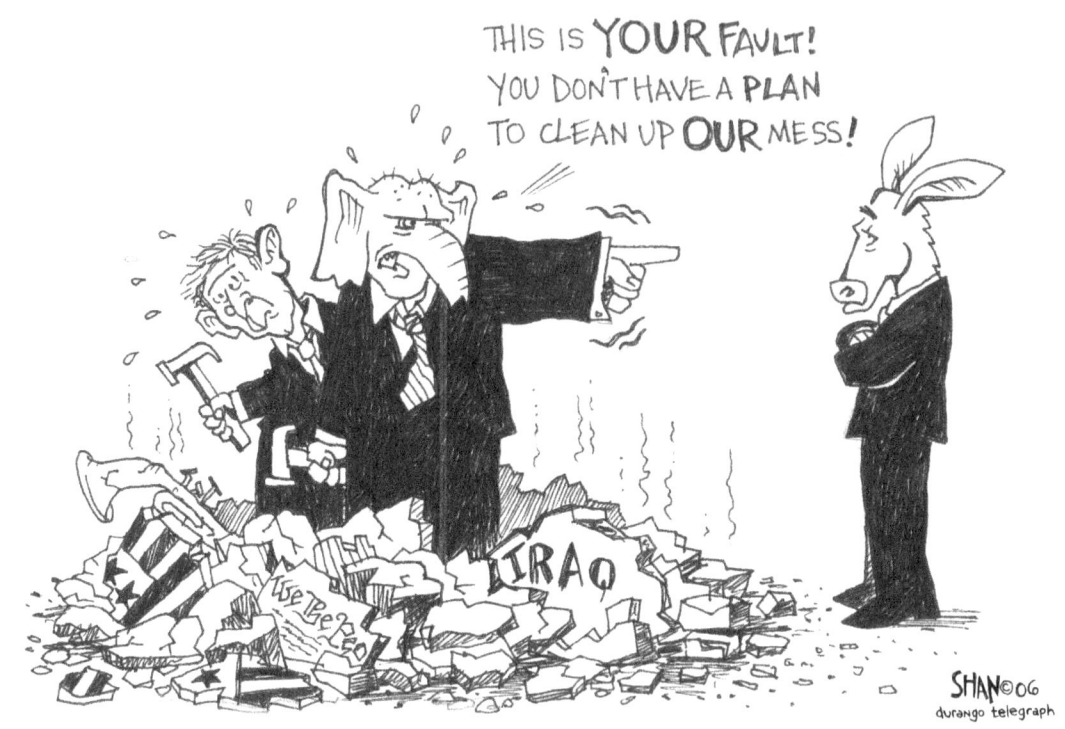

Although change had come to America in the midterms, power over the wars still rested primarily with the Bush Administration. Congressional Republicans were unwilling to compromise on any sort of withdrawal, all the while attempting to blame the nation's problems on newly installed Democratic majorities.

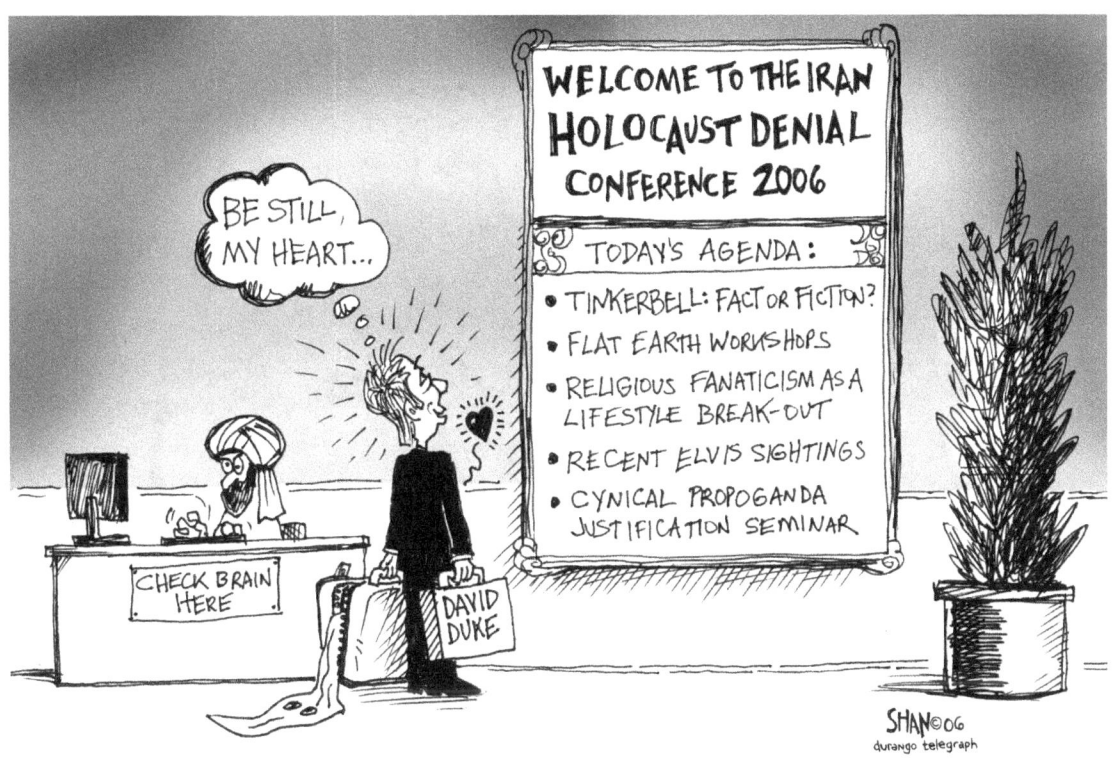

Iran's president, Mahmoud Ahmadinejad, is a frequent Holocaust denier. In a 2005 speech he said,

> "They have fabricated a legend, under the name Massacre of the Jews, and they hold it higher than God himself, religion itself and the prophets themselves...If somebody in their country questions God, nobody says anything, but if somebody denies the myth of the massacre of Jews, the Zionist loudspeakers and the governments in the pay of Zionism will start to scream."

Former American Nazi and KKK Grand Wizard, David Duke's pathetic denier stance on the Holocaust made a perfect segue for speaking about the hateful tripe Iran's president used for logic.

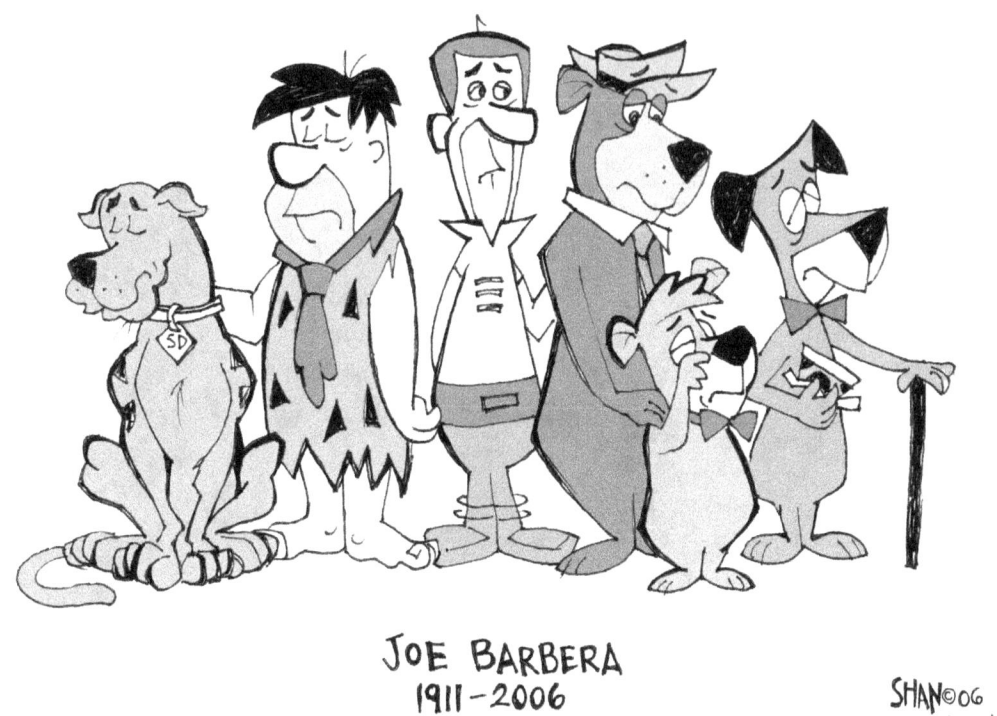

JOE BARBERA
1911-2006

SHAN©06
durango telegraph

Joe Barbera was the other half of the immensely talented and successful animation studio, Hanna-Barbera. The studio invented many of the twentieth century's most beloved cartoon characters, including *Scooby Doo, The Flintstones, The Jetsons, Yogi Bear,* and *Huckleberry Hound.*

I loved those shows as a kid, and adored the memory of them as an adult. While they will live on for decades as reruns, drawing these characters for such a cartoon felt just like a funeral.

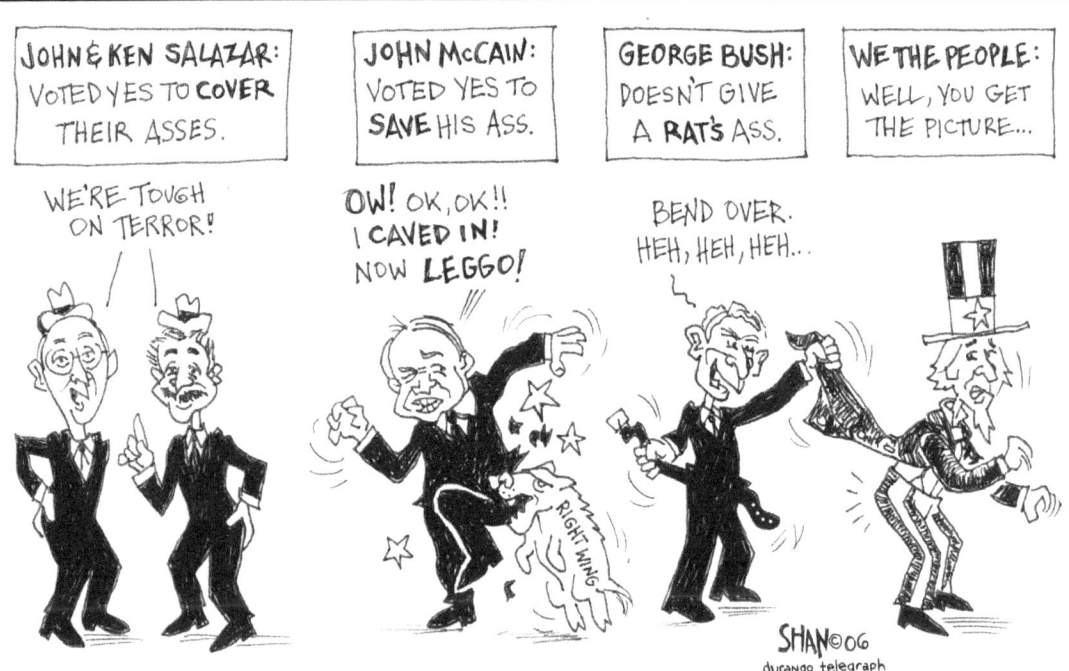

One of the last acts of the GOP before their November "thumpin' was to pass the Military Commissions Act. Also known as the "Torture Bill." The act's ostensible purpose was to "authorize trial by military commission for violations of the law of war." In actuality, it was an unconstitutional encroachment on habeas corpus, allowing the government to label any citizen an "unlawful combatant," then lock them away without due process for years.

Fortunately, the Supreme Court ruled against the law, and set up a process for Federal Courts to hear petitions, but not before several legislators, including John McCain and my elective representatives showed their political cowardice and voted it into law.

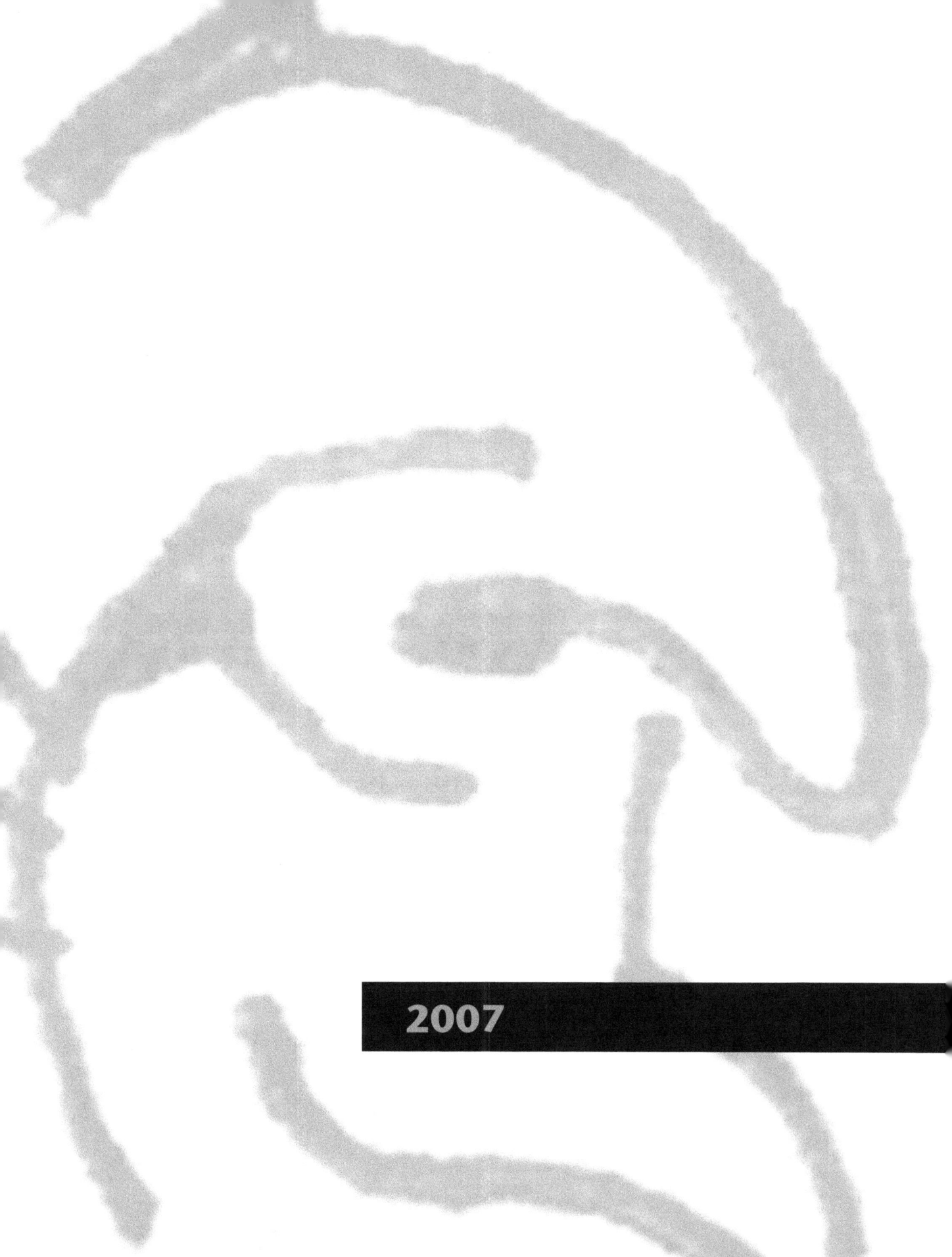

2007

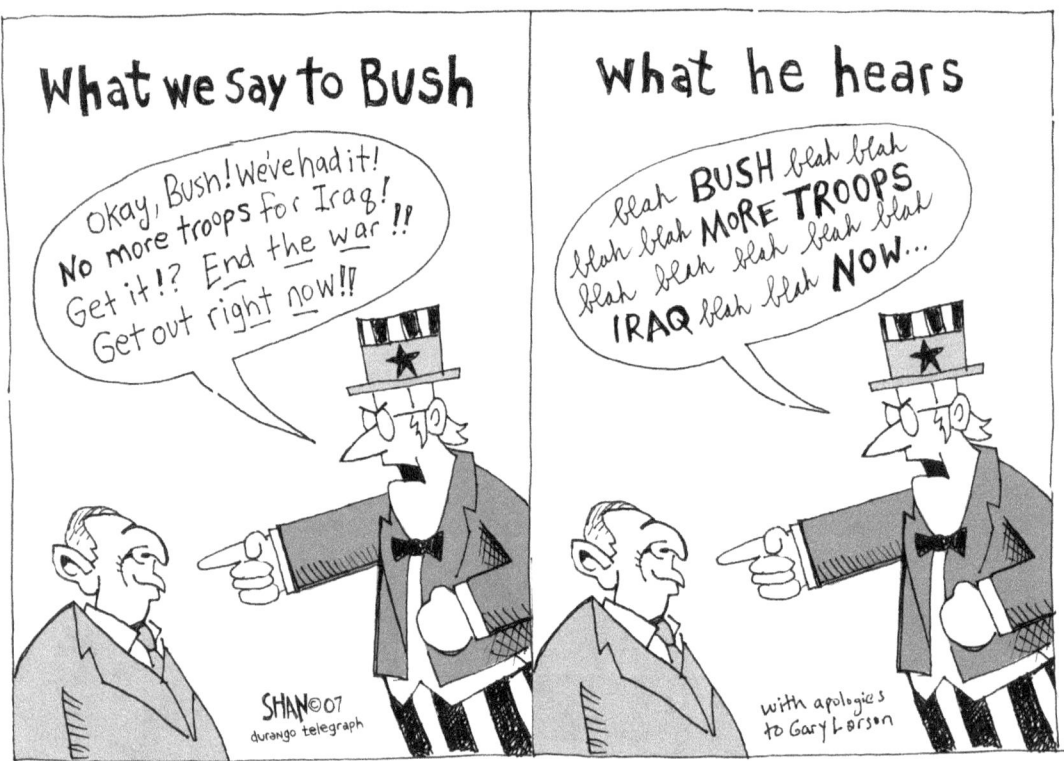

One thing that never changed in the Bush years was the absolute certainty with which the Great Decider pursued his ideology. He never seemed bothered by the destruction of Iraq, our military, the economy, New Orleans, US credibility, torture bills, or any of the other great disasters that sprang to life from his brow like some twisted Athena.

In this vein, I conceived as Bush as a vacuous *Far Side* character. Gary Larson was one of the greatest 20th century cartoonists, and no one could draw the intellectually challenged better. So I borrowed a bit of his style, and was absolutely shocked how easy it was to construct a Larson-style W.

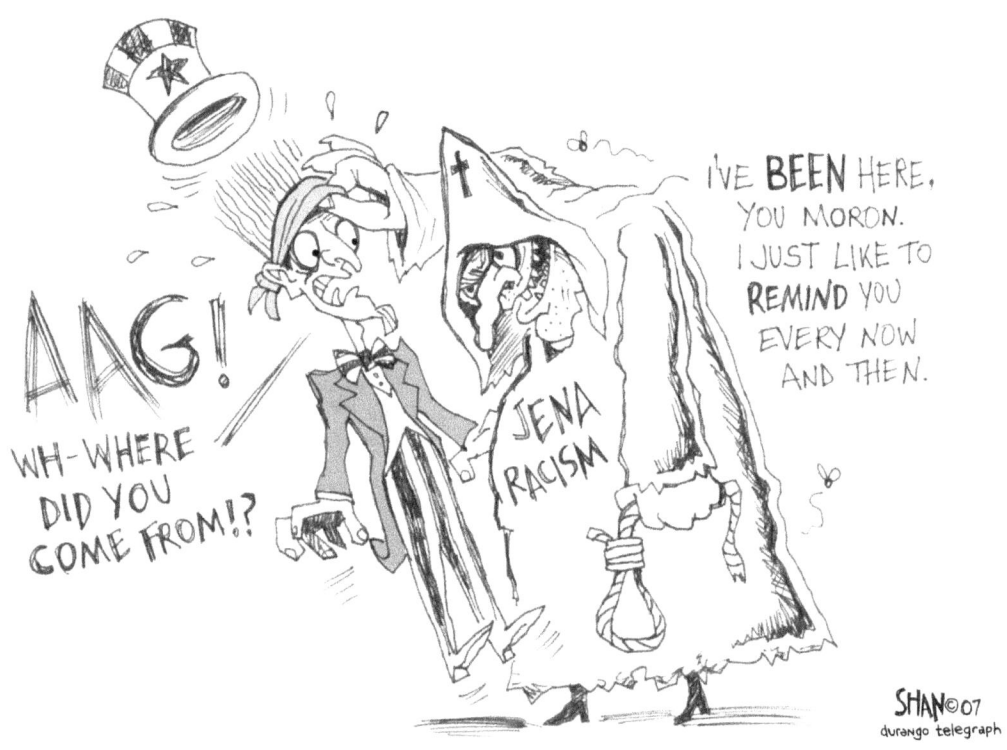

Jena High School in is in Jena, Louisiana. In December of 2006, six black teens were convicted of beating a white student after a series of increasing serious altercations fomented by racial tensions.

The problems started after a group of black kids sat under a tree in the school courtyard that was known as the "white tree." The next day, nooses were discovered swinging from the branches.

After all hell broke loose, the school convened an investigative committee, who almost unbelievably determined that the kids who put them there had "no knowledge that nooses symbolize the terrible legacy of the lynchings of countless blacks in American history."

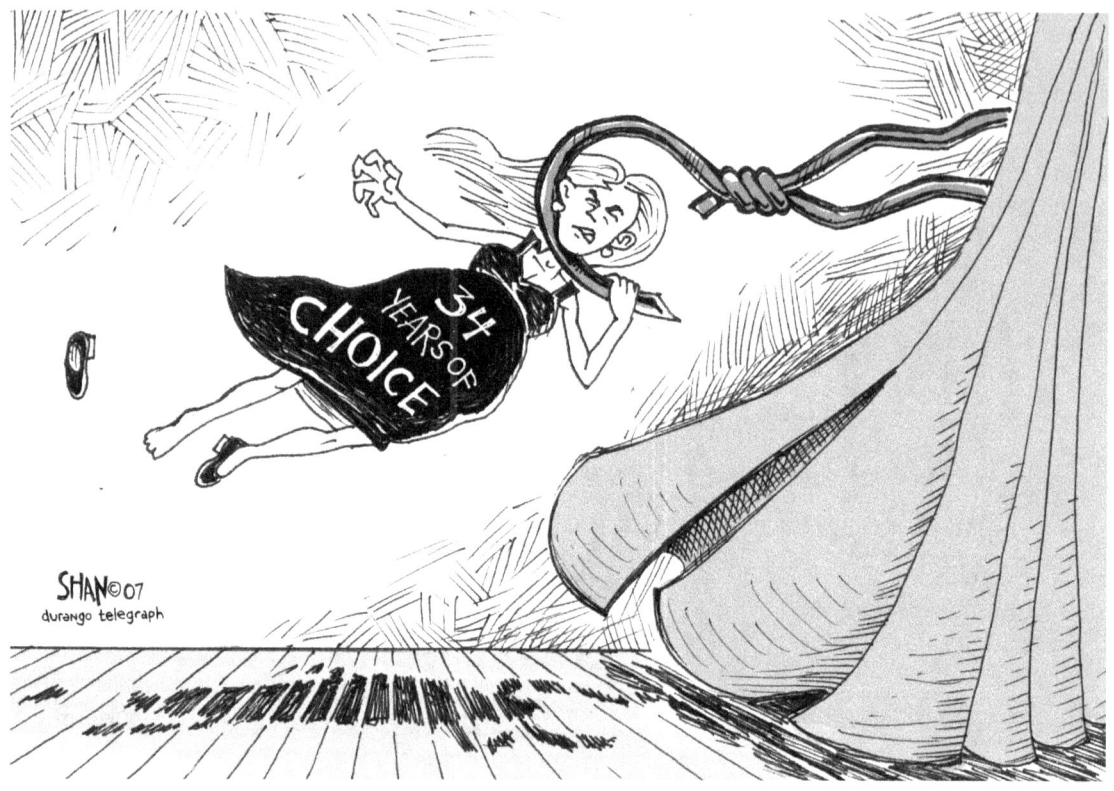

The Supreme Court has, with the two conservative appointments of Alito and Roberts made by Bush, swung wildly to the right. In 2007, the court ruled, 5 to 4, that the Partial-bIrth Abortion Ban Act, signed in 2003, was Constitutionally legal in banning the right of women to have such a procedure, except in the case of a life-threatening complication. There was no provision to protect the health of women.

Abortion is a tragedy. To force a woman to have a baby against her will is even more so. And yet the religious right refuses to even entertain the idea of sexuality among teens, and so lobbies for no sexual education except abstinence, and presumably, prayer. Besides being a strategy set firmly in the 1920's, their approach flies in the face of millions of years of evolution. Demanding strict enforcement of neutered, non-sexual world-view, (especially in young people), is about as effective as throwing rocks to knock the moon from the sky.

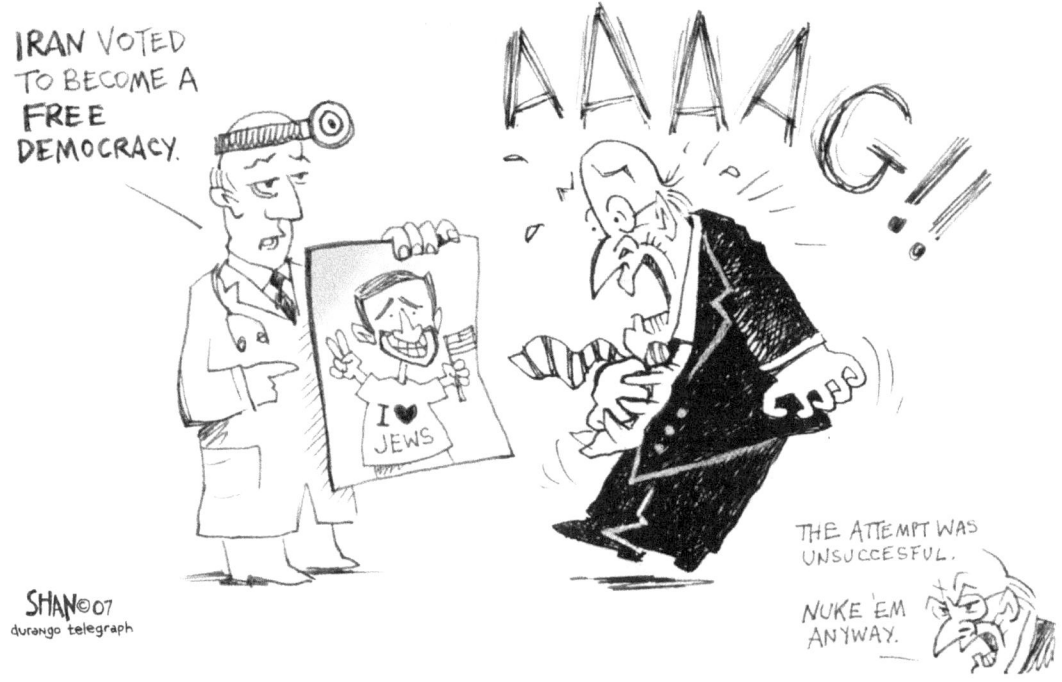

Occasionally, aging politicians have surgery for some ailment, and cartoonists use the opportunity to make a joke. In this case, Vice President Dick Cheney, an unfortunate victim of multiple heart attacks, had some therapy for his ticker. I couldn't resist the irony.

Cheney was infamous for his callousness. He once shot a friend in the face while bird hunting, and never apologized. In fact, one of the Veep's favorite sports was "hunting," here defined as: "having your man release 500 domesticated pen raised pheasants from a cage so that you and your buddies can blast 417 of them to bits." Dead-eye Dick killed over 70 of them himself.

Imagine having not only the absolute absence of anything resembling sportsmanship, but the even more disturbing characteristic of enjoying, indeed, orchestrating, an act of mass killing. One is reminded of a cat slowly disemboweling a mouse, an oily purr resonating through the settee.

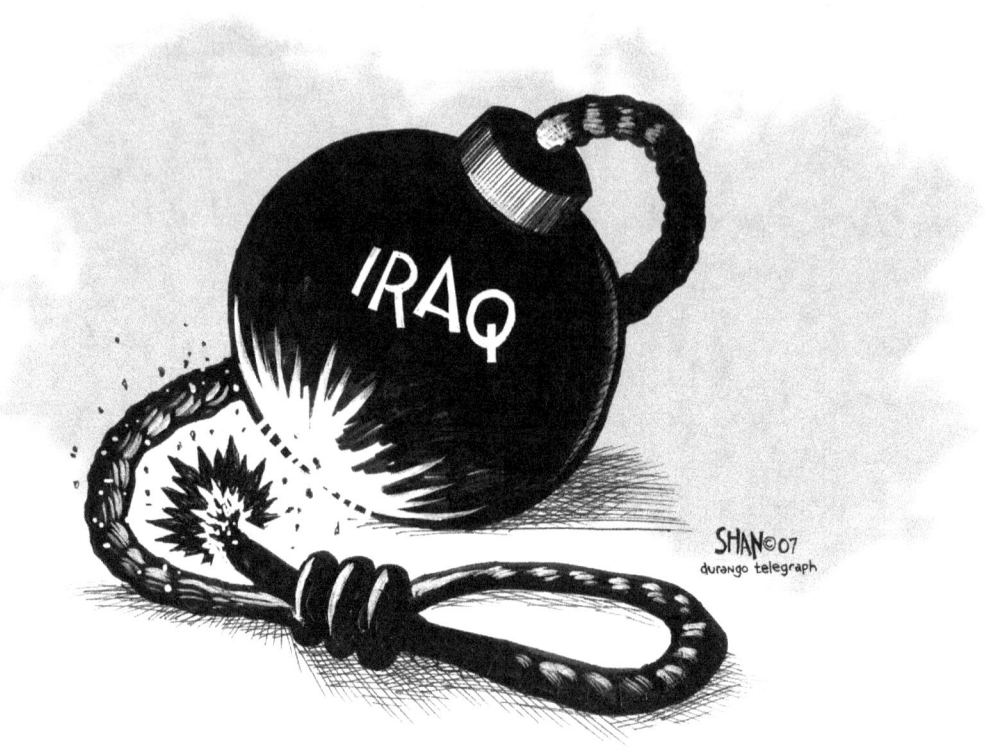

Saddam Hussein was executed by hanging in December of 2006. The execution was violent, undignified, and bitter. Shi'a hangmen mocked the former Iraqi dictator before stretching his neck.

Like many at the time, I was worried abut Iraq exploding into factional chaos as the hanging was conducted just before *Eid al-Adha*, a Sunni Muslim celebration. Saddam was a Sunni. The ultimate reaction was factional, as predicted, but more muted than was feared.

This work marked the first time I used a stylus, or digital drawing tool, to create the flaring effects on the fuse and the bomb, and the background neutral tone.

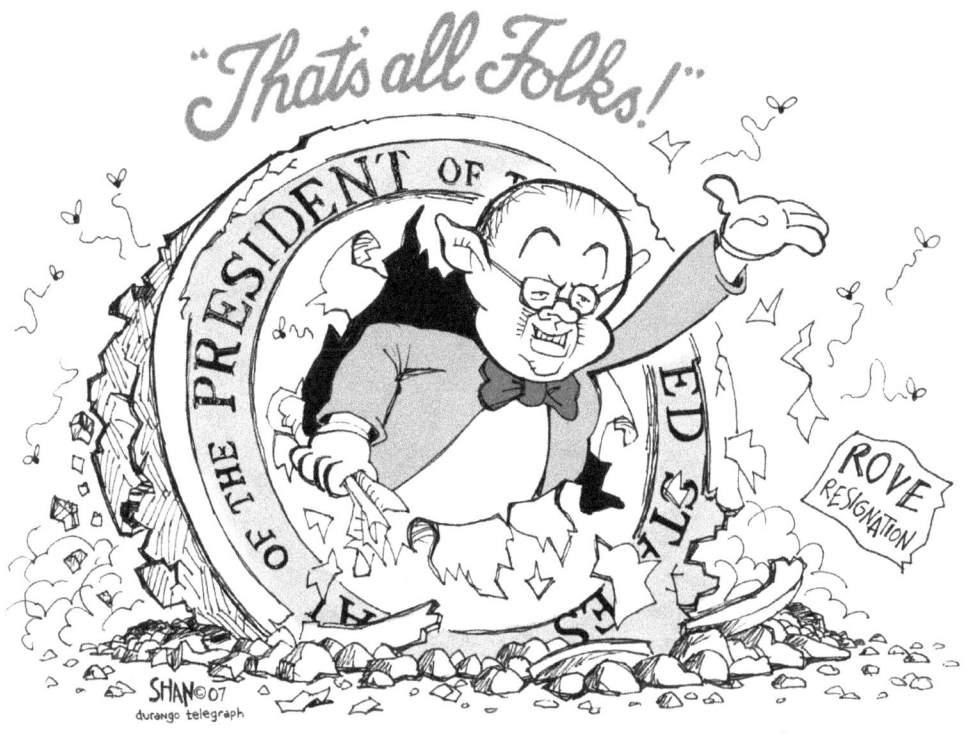

"That's all Folks!"

ROVE RESIGNATION

SHAN©07
durango telegraph

Carl Rove was easily one of the most cynical, cunning and dangerous Republican apparatchiks ever to slime forth from under the great glistening regressive rock. His tenure under Bush was vicious and petty, but he did his job better than anyone around at the time.

Rove's great innovation was to attack his opponent's strength rather than his weaknesses. Seems obvious now, but the latter strategy was the norm up until Rove took the field. He destroyed Al Gore in 2000 by using the VP's global warming advocacy to paint him as a wonkish nutball. Rove then eviscerated John Kerry in the 2004 elections by going after his credentials as a war hero. By the time Rove was through, Kerry, twice awarded the Purple Heart for service in Vietnam, was seen as an un-American traitor. G.W. Bush, who spent the Vietnam war stateside and possible AWOL from the cushy "favorite son" Texas Air National Guard post procured for him by Daddy Bush, was a seen as a war hero.

Horrible, but impressive.

Rove resigned after the "thumpin" of 2006, when the GOP lost 51 House seats to insurgent Democrats, his juju temporarily spent. The guy's balding resemblance to Porky Pig, a famous Warner Bros. cartoon character who closed every *Looney Tunes* cartoon with a "The-Tha-The-Tha-The-That's all, folks!" was too good a joke not to exploit.

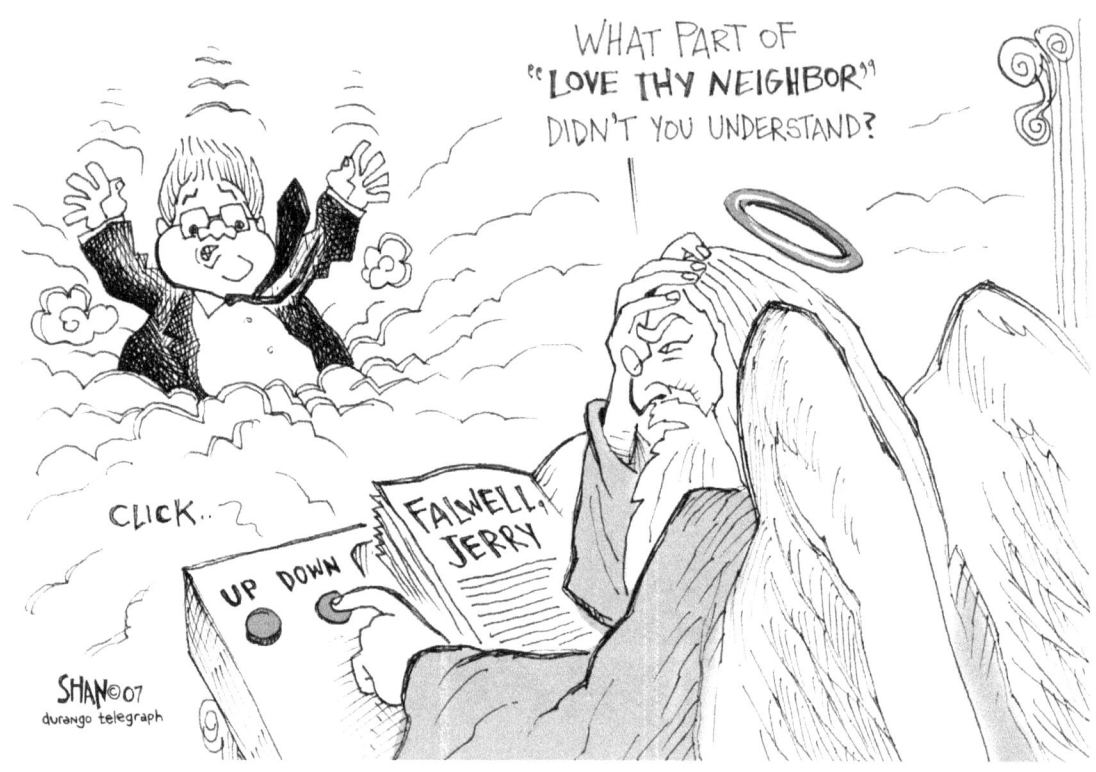

The Reverend Jerry Falwell was an unequivocal dick. I will illustrate the immensity of his dickishness in bullet points below:

• Founder of Moral Majority, responsible for electing Reagan by delivering the dick vote.
• Founder of Liberty "University," where young regressives are taught evolution is wrong.
• Regularly featured segregationist dicks like George Wallace on his 1960's-era radio show.
• Advocated getting rid of public education and replacing it with Evangelical Christian teaching.
• Supported apartheid, calling Noble Peace Prize winner Desmond Tutu a "phony."
• Created video "documentaries" asserting President Bill Clinton was murderer.
• Condemned homosexuality, quoting "Gay people would just as soon kill you as look at you."
• Blamed the 9/11 attacks on "...the pagans, and the abortionists, and the feminists, and the gays and the lesbians..."
• Opined that Muhammad was a terrorist
• Claimed that a Twinky Winky the Teletubby was intended as a gay role model because he carried a purse.

Jerry Falwell was a dick.

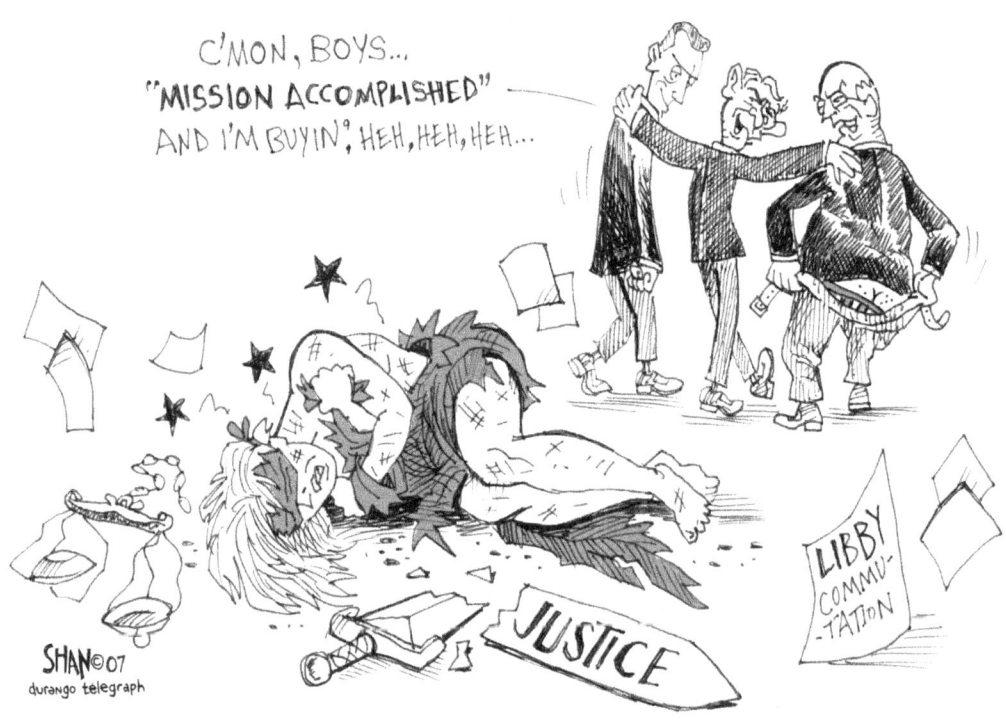

The long, convoluted and seriously messed-up story of Scooter Libby, Dick Cheney and their unbeleivable, illegal outing of CIA agent Valerie Plame Wilson in order to discredit her husband, former ambassador Robert Wilson, is too long a tale for this volume. Google it, if you please, to appreciate the immensity of the disservice done to justice.

My worry with this piece was that it was too brutal. I especially wanted to show Lady Liberty post-rape as exposed without being titillating, which would be as sick as the act itself.

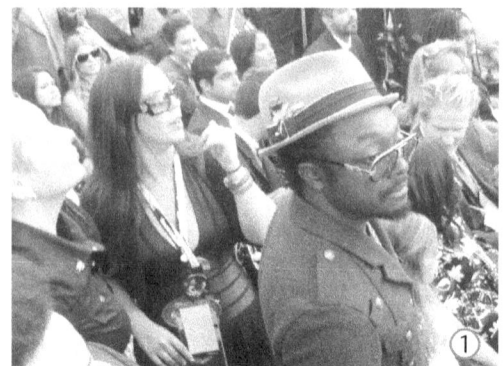

In the spring of 2008, I approached the Durango Telegraph's *Jefe's* with a plan to travel to Denver for the purpose of covering the Democratic National Convention. It was a once in a lifetime opportunity to be on the ground when the first black President was nominated.

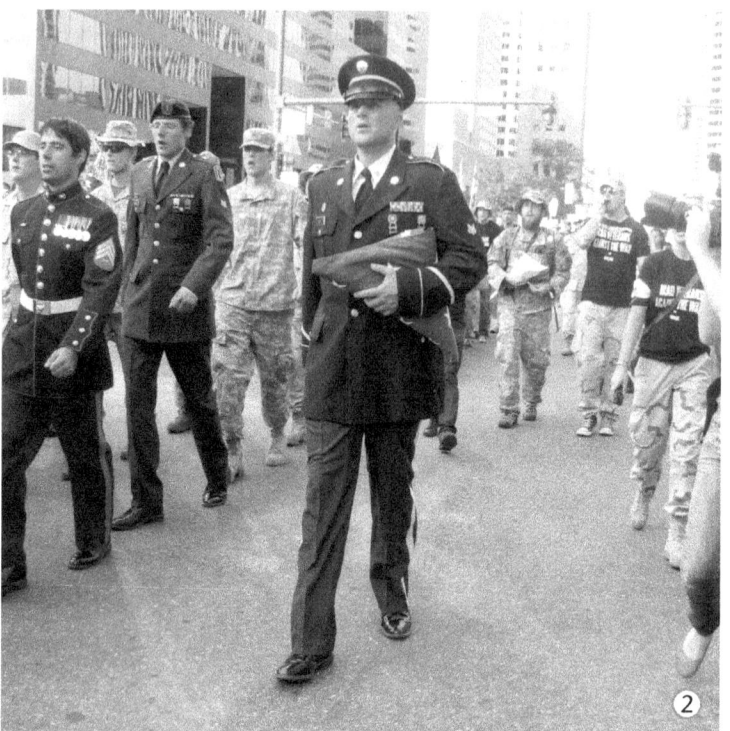

My intent was to cover the convention not from the political angle, but as a "backstage" point of view whith a little gonzo first person thrown in, complete with accompanying cartoon portraits of the more charismatic participants. I was after the little things...the granular substance of political spectacle.

It was not a disappointment. The thing I remember most aside from the crush of people and ideologies, was the pregnant air of possibility.

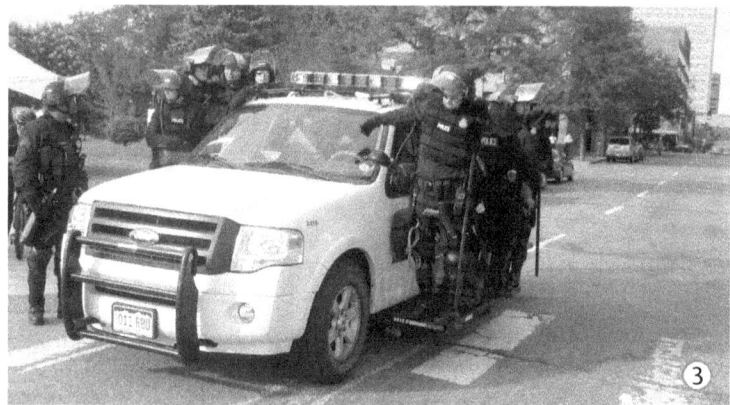

Black, white, young, old...we all convened post hoc panels aboard the trains going home each night, giddily expounding about the new paradigm we were midwifing, the palpable sense of history aborning.

For the first and only time in my life, I felt a kinship with strangers that bordered on the familial.

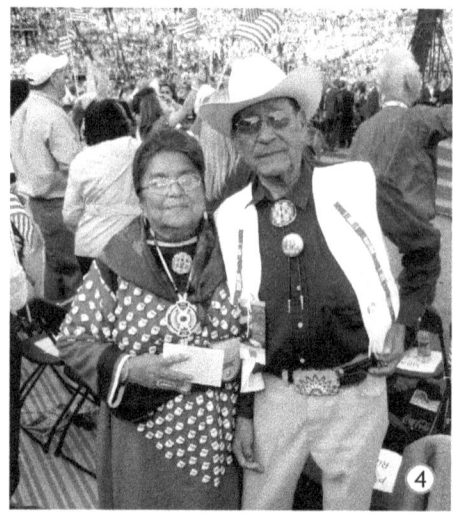

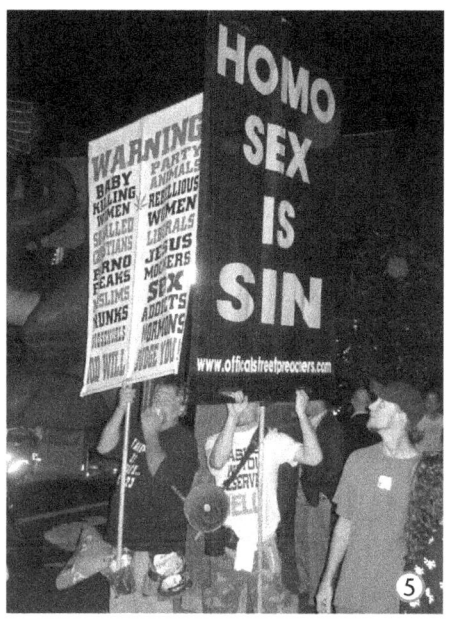

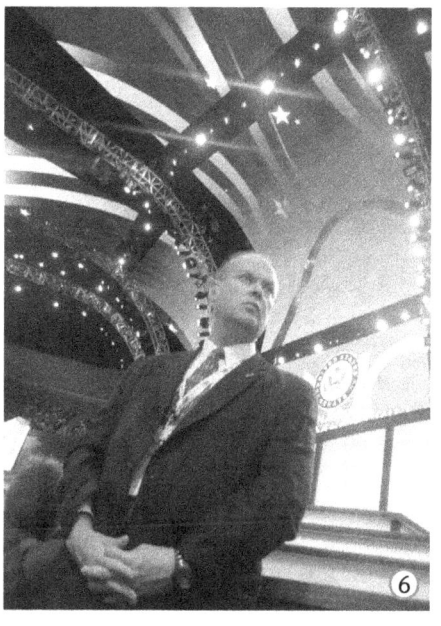

1. Celebrities amongst the crowd at Invesco Stadium

2. Veterans march through downtown Denver in an anti-war protest

3. SWAT teams hover in the background of a peace march

4. Native American delegates

5. Westboro Baptist Church members in full voice

6. Security at the Pepsi Center Stage

7. Shan at the convention

8. Barack Obama at Invesco Stadium

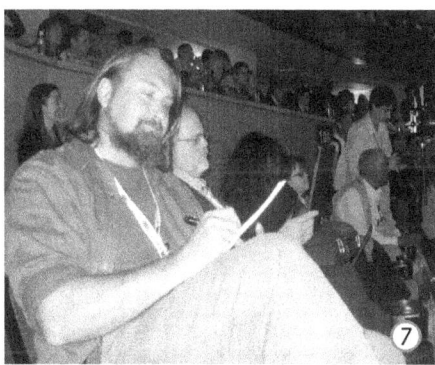

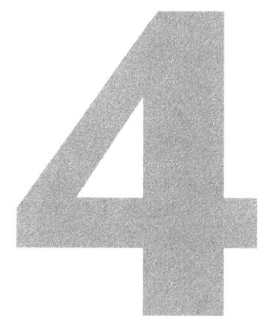

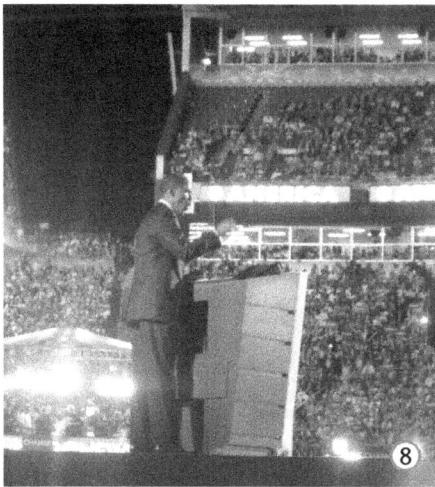

4
DAYS
IN
DENVER

2008 democratic national convention

• Three idling ambulances are lined up next to the Pepsi Center. They are flanked by a Trojans Condoms display, manned by young women enthusiastically giving out bright yellow samples emblazoned with "EVOLVE." Later on, someone hands me a condom printed with the words, "Protect Yourself from John McCain." No need for bumper stickers-prophylactics are the vehicle of choice for sloganeering this year.

• The Secret Service folks are all incredibly nondescript. Almost all are skinny white Ed Norton look-a likes wearing flak vests and high-holstered Gloks. No doubt they could break me with their pinky, but it's a blow to my preconceived notions.

• Within the hall, most of the Delegate seats are empty, except for Delaware. Freshly moved to the front of the line after Obama tapped Biden for Veep, the group is in full song whilst tossing around three beachballs. Even the dustiest state comptroller speeches have the Delegates hooting like teens at a Springsteen concert.

• Downtown on the 16th street mall, the big boys have come to play. These are professional haters who have balls big enough to scream, "God hates fags!" at military funerals. I'm not enough of a challenge for them to even notice, but I do my best, and wind up almost getting into a fight anyway. After their group is ringed by a tense wall of SWAT cops wearing enough weaponry to invade a small county, I decide that those dusty comptroller speeches back at the Convention weren't so boring after all. The area is bad for the health of those easily enraged.

• Pepsi Center Hall fills rapidly as the evening approaches, with its promise of remarks from Democratic luminaries. Unable to figure out where the press box is, I'm forced up into the nosebleed seats in order to have some room for my elbows. My neighbor and I decide that the seat between us is taken. And it is. By our elbows. Amazingly, the seat stays unoccupied and continues that way all night, right up to the point my conscience compels me to offer the empty chair to a couple sitting on the steps next to me, while I head down to the main floor.

• A gallery of network pundits are in full view, speaking from small stages filled with cameras and futuristic touch-screens, around which the milling crowd swirls and eddies. Randomly, I notice three things: James Carville is wearing yellow jogging shoes, Katie Couric looks remarkably glum when she's not on camera, and Anderson Cooper is a very tiny albino doll-man.

• The hall is arranged so that the major news networks have filming platforms that jut out into the almost vertical surrounding seats, like neon cliff dwellings. The BBC, Telemundo, Canadian Broadcasting, Al Jazeera...it seems the whole world is indeed watching. Fox News, directly below me, is having trouble keeping their set carpeting attached to the floorboards. Looks like their rug is being pulled...

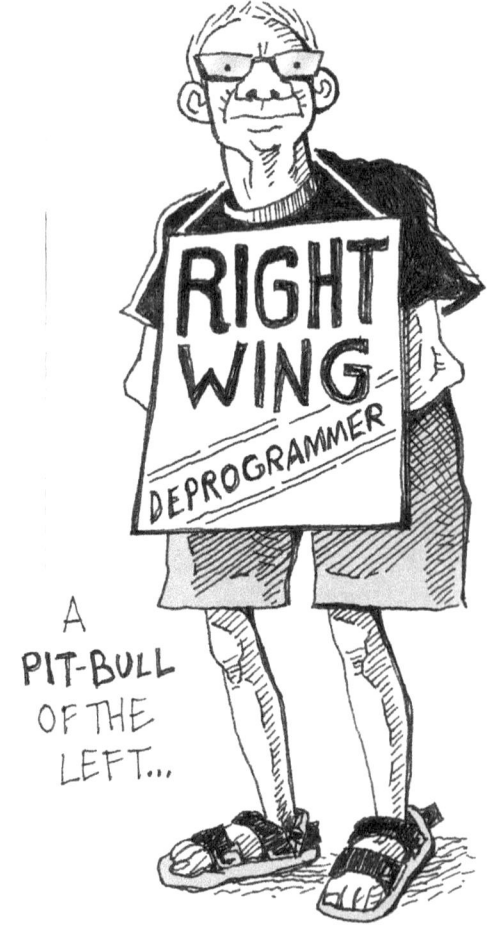

A PIT-BULL OF THE LEFT...

• Noticing the huge divide between what's going on in the hall and what the networks are saying, I tap the guy in front of me to ask if he's been to many conventions and if they're all like this. He agrees with me that the coverage is skewed. I realize I'm talking to Spike Lee. Loathe to actually ask for a souvenir shot, I surreptitiously photograph the back of his head.

• Gradually it dawns on me that it's possible to swap out my upper section credentials for a floor pass that can be kept for 45 minutes. I decide to get in line for this treat at roughly the time Hillary Clinton's being cued up to speak, which turns out to be a lucky move. All access to the hall is abruptly shut down by the fire marshals. Consequentially, the floor pass is mine for the night. A reporter from the Dallas Morning News and I slap an evil high five, celebrating half of our colleagues being shut out of the most important speech of the convention.

• A small, balding man in an expensive suit shoots pass me in the corridor. My body reacts strangely, hands clenching in a short spasm of anger. In the few seconds it takes my brain to catch up, baldy dives into the Fox News box. It's Karl Rove. His aura apparently promotes reflexive acts of bodily assault by liberals.

• The real heros of the Convention are the staffers that distribute placards during the key speeches. Although the floor is insanely crowded, they slide through as if greased. Their dispersions are impeccably timed. Clinton's appearance triggers an avalanche of white "Hillary" signs, which are just as quickly replaced with "Unity" flags. In short order, the pit is a swarming mass of red, white and blue slogans. Mission accomplished, sides heaving, the sign slingers retire to the eves in preparation for the next rhetorical onslaught .

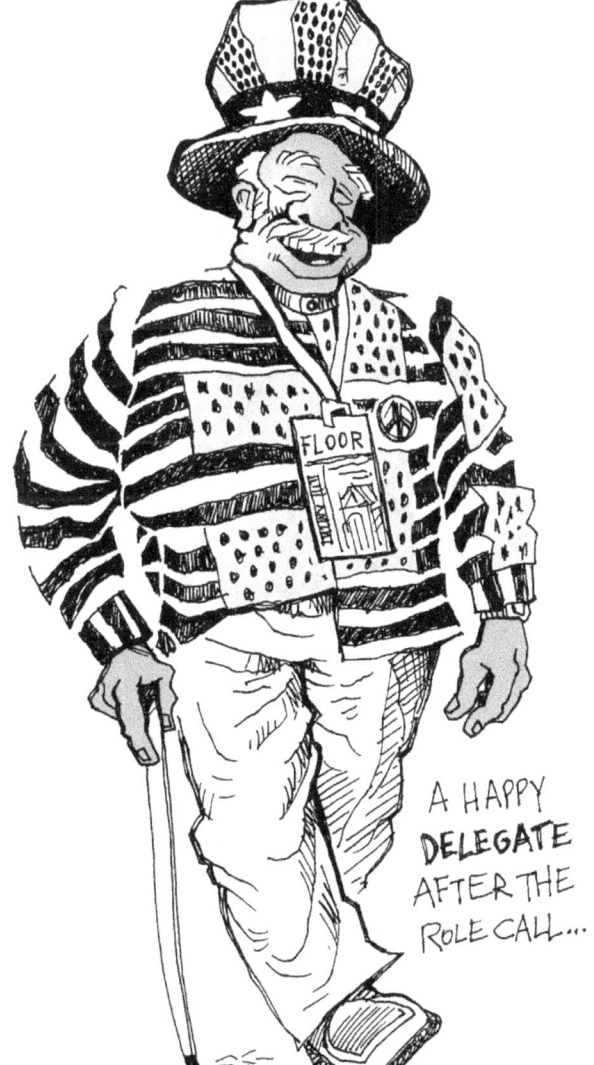

A HAPPY DELEGATE AFTER THE ROLE CALL...

• Onstage, a man with wounded eyes from Michigan is telling us how he lost his job and insurance, and was diagnosed with diabetes. Few are listening. On the nearby steps a be-suited local anchorman begins a four-take monologue about the delegates' costumes. "There you have it, everything from masks to tambourines tonight at the Pepsi Center!" Meanwhile, Michigan man finishes his somber tale, and limps off the stage to scattered applause. It's rough symbolizing a shitty economy. Even the people on your side don't really want to hear about it.

81

• An open air art installation graces the sidewalk on the way into the Pepsi Center. I stop to have a look. The City of Denver commissioned several politically themed projects for the Convention, and this is one of the best I've seen. Taking each President's State of the Union Speech, artist Luke Dubois culled out the most repeated words and set them up like an eye chart, listing the most used word as the largest, one for all of our commander-in-chiefs. Bush's chart starts with "terror" as the largest word. Nixon's most used word was "truly." The effect is brilliant: US history in a paragraph.

Here are the top words in order, 1790- 2008:

Gentlemen, France, Limits, Enemy, Parties, Mutual, Bank, Results, Texas, Oregon, Empire, Deem, Central, Slavery, Emancipation, Republican, Products, Coinage, Likely, Treatment, Wages, Resolve, Puerto, Corporations, Procedure, Processes, Relationship, Veterans, Unemployment, Democratic, Soviet, Nuclear, Alliance, Tonight, Truly, Barrels, Us, Deficits, Idea, 21st, Terror.

• I decide to brave the protest circus again, and am not disappointed. Almost immediately I stumble onto a huge peace protest, led by dozens of vets against the war. The usual black-armored riot police are omnipresent, but one cop looks strangely out of place. She is at least a foot and a half shorter than her peers. I want to ask her a question, but I instinctively fear her, and so settle for a quick picture. What kind of total bad-ass would you have to be to make the SWAT team as a four foot-eight woman?

• The theme of imminent riot is continued as I funnel into the Convention entrance, now reduced to one checkpoint due to the chanting marchers rumbling by barely a block away. Clusters of armored assault cops are poised in tight packs, raised helmet shields accentuating the rapacious attention they're paying the protestors. Walking between the two groups feels reckless. I'm disturbingly reminded of lions watching wildebeest, eyes wide and glistening.

• The last night of the DNC at the Pepsi Center is slightly nostalgic, as the whole shebang gets shipped to Invesco Stadium for the finale on Thursday. Demand for souvenirs is high. Press and Delegates alike strip the hall of anything that can be reasonably carried off, leaving the place looking more than a little tattered.

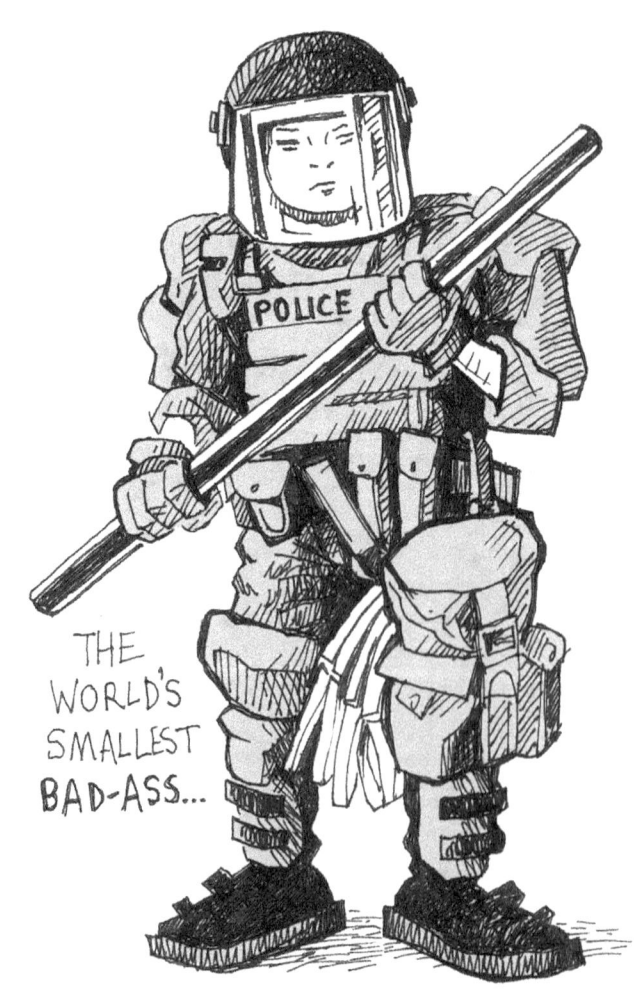

THE WORLD'S SMALLEST BAD-ASS...

• Invesco Stadium is considerably easier to get into than the Pepsi Center, if you don't count the extra wait for the High Line public transit being shut down by protesters. Forced to disembark two miles from the site, I walk down a blocked-off central Denver cloverleaf towards the massive stadium. Tens of thousands walk with me along the great empty asphalt loop, a pilgrimage of modern times complete with the devout and the doubters, costumes, music, and artifacts.

• Through a combination of blind luck and persistence, I quickly find a way inside. The floor is much larger than the Pepsi Center, but even more crowded, as the networks have erected broadcasting platforms so large that the previous islands of punditry at the Pepsi Center seem amateurish tree-houses by comparison. The main stage, a faux greek colonnade, commands the space. Nearby, an NPR reporter describes the structure as similar to Caesars Palace. I find it strange that a seasoned Beltway journalist is unable to recognize the architectural symbol for Democracy.

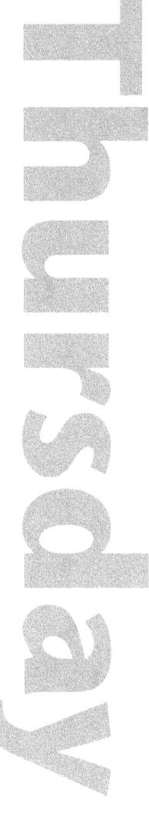

• Finding a safe space is difficult. The fire marshals are vigilant. Everywhere I stand is only good for a few minutes before I get shooed along. Eventually I locate a good spot twenty feet from the podium. When Obama makes his appearance the crowd's roar and stamping is so loud that it triggers primal terror, causing me to forcefully resist dropping into a fight or flight crouch. The candidate finishes, and a wind cannon behind me fires off a dazzling burst of confetti streamers, knocking my hair into my eyes. A blizzard of floating paper color surrounds us, mixed with the pop of fireworks and heartfelt declarations of the Delegates, many of whom are openly weeping. This display causes a feeding frenzy among the assembled media, their hand-cam spotlights weaving to and fro, hot for the humanity of the moment.

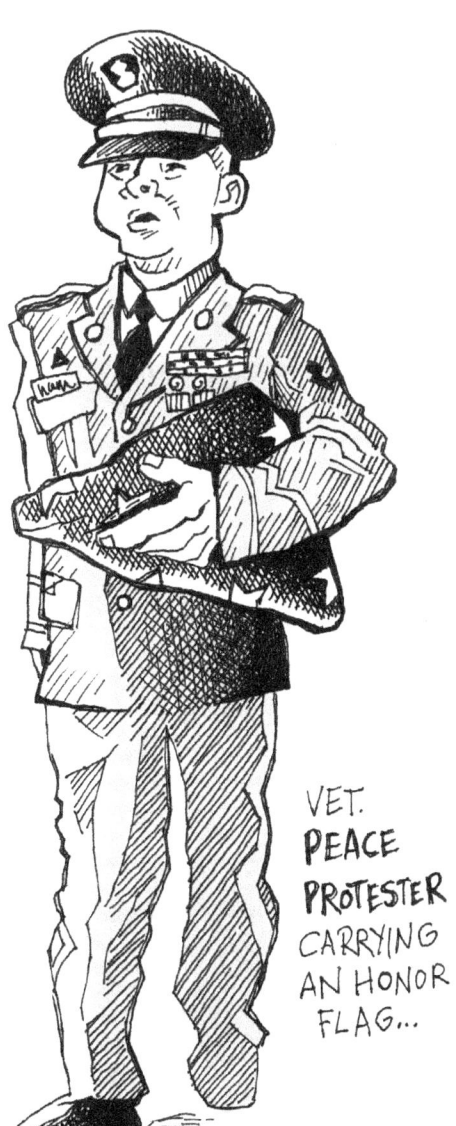

VET.
PEACE
PROTESTER
CARRYING
AN HONOR
FLAG...

• With a final wave and a roar, it's done. The crowd flows out and away. Every night of the convention I've collected partisan souvenirs, but tonight I have a small US flag. It is a symbol that resists being appropriated too long by any one group or ideology, because it belongs to us all. In the past, I've denigrated flag-waving as a xenophobic exercise, but holding the cheap little wood and cloth construction in my hand, I see I was wrong. Tonight's flags were for the oppressed and the invisible, for joy and peace, and for a constant renewal of what makes us truly a people: the ability to transcend our differences and work together. We've had fear and anger for the better part of a decade, and perhaps that's why Obama can conjure up 80,000 people to hear him speak. He reminds us of our better angels, and what we could do if we dare to try.

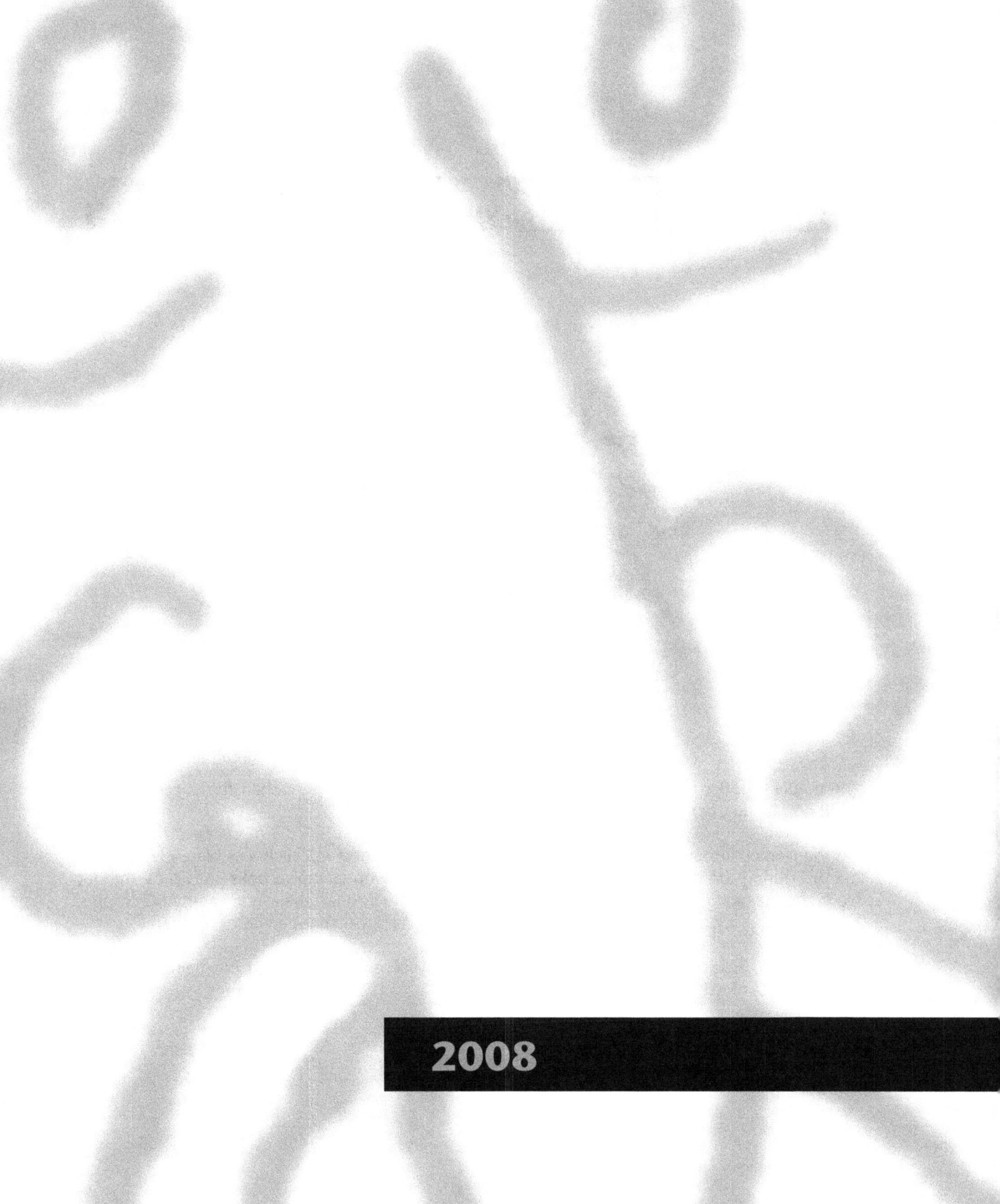

2008

EQUAL OPPORTUNITY CENSORSHIP

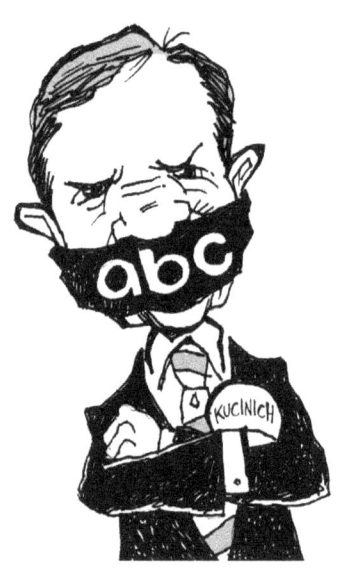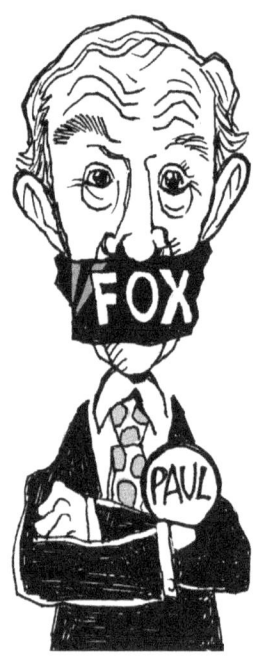

The media's modern role as kingmaker was no more readily apparent than the coverage of the 2008 nomination battles for President.

On the Democratic side, longtime progressive champion Dennis Kucinich was blatantly censored by ABC during the debates. The Cleveland Congressman won both live polls put up by the network, despite being asked only one question, 2/3 of the way through the event. Later, ABC cropped Kucinich out of a photograph of all 8 hopefuls, making it appear that he was never there.

In GOP land, Texas Libertarian Ron Paul was similarly censored, including not being invited to a FOX debate of the candidates.

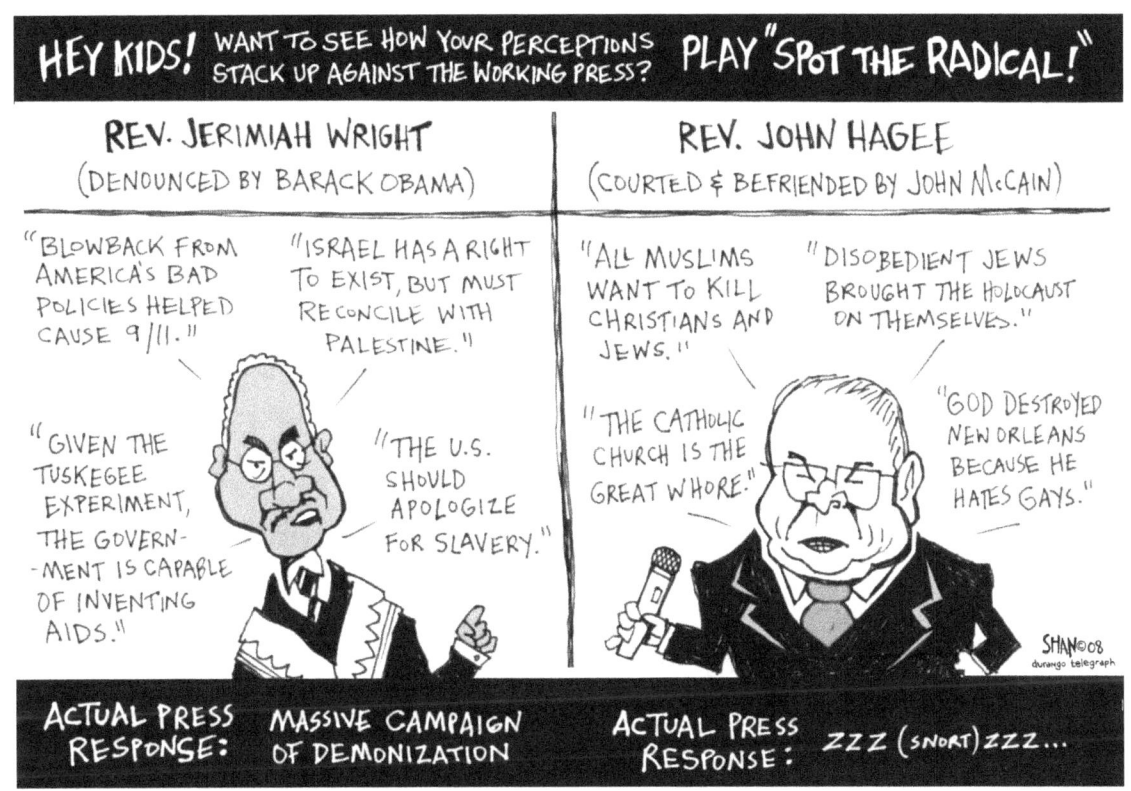

As Barack Obama's candidacy became a viable concern, more serious attempts were made to derail the future President's candidacy. Once included an attempt to smear Obama as a black racist. The pastor of Obama's Chicago church, Jerimiah Wright, is a Black Liberation Theologian, and had made several blunt statements on tape prior to 2008. These recordings were released and used by the right as evidence that Obama could not be trusted to impartially represent all Americans. Obama was forced to distance himself from the Minster. After Wright gave a fiery speech defending himself before the NAACP, the candidate resigned from his church, denouncing Wright's assertions.

What seemed to go whistling right past the media's attention in all this was the Rev. John Haggee, who played a similar role in Republican John McCain's campaign. The only difference was that Wright's comments, though brash, were for the most part grounded in reality, whereas Hagee's comments could only charitably be called lunatic.

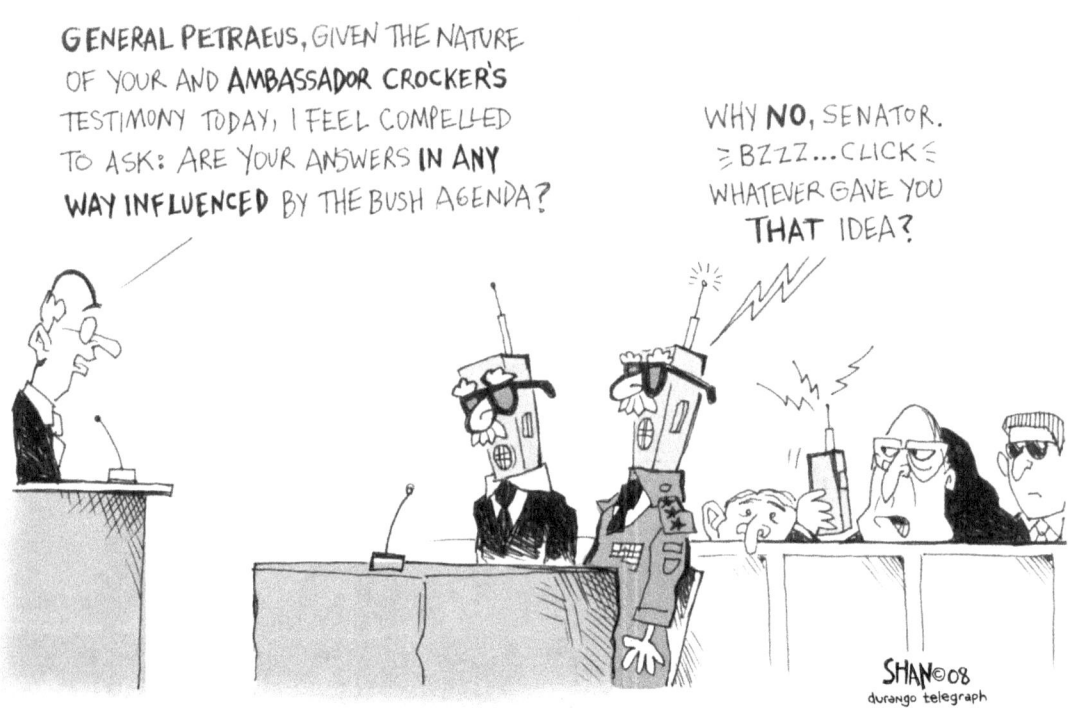

General David Petraeus was perhaps the most successful of the principle military figures of the Iraq War, surviving well into the Obama Administration and eventually taking over the war in Afghanistan. In 2008, his hearings before the United States Senate Committee on Armed Services and the United States Senate Committee on Foreign Relations fueled speculation that the US would be going into Iran next.

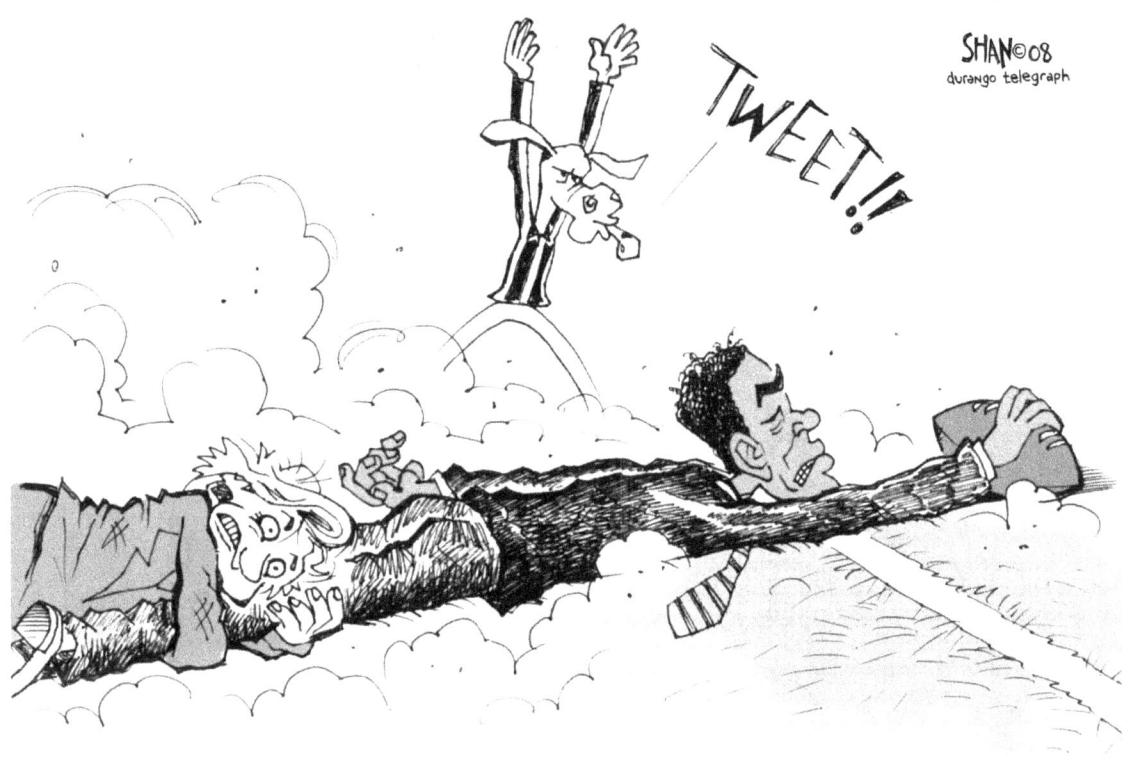

The struggle for the Democratic nomination for President between former First Lady and New York Senator Hillary Clinton, and Illinois Senator Barack Obama was epic. The race split the Democratic constituency down the middle and vastly increased turnout in the primaries. I lost friends over the rupture. Even now I wonder if I backed the right horse.

At the time I worried about the dynastic qualities of a Bush/Clinton/Bush/Clinton sequence. With hindsight, it's clear that Hillary would have been much more of a "gloves off" combatant than Obama. If the President is unable to escape his doomed obsession with bipartisanship, she may yet get her chance.

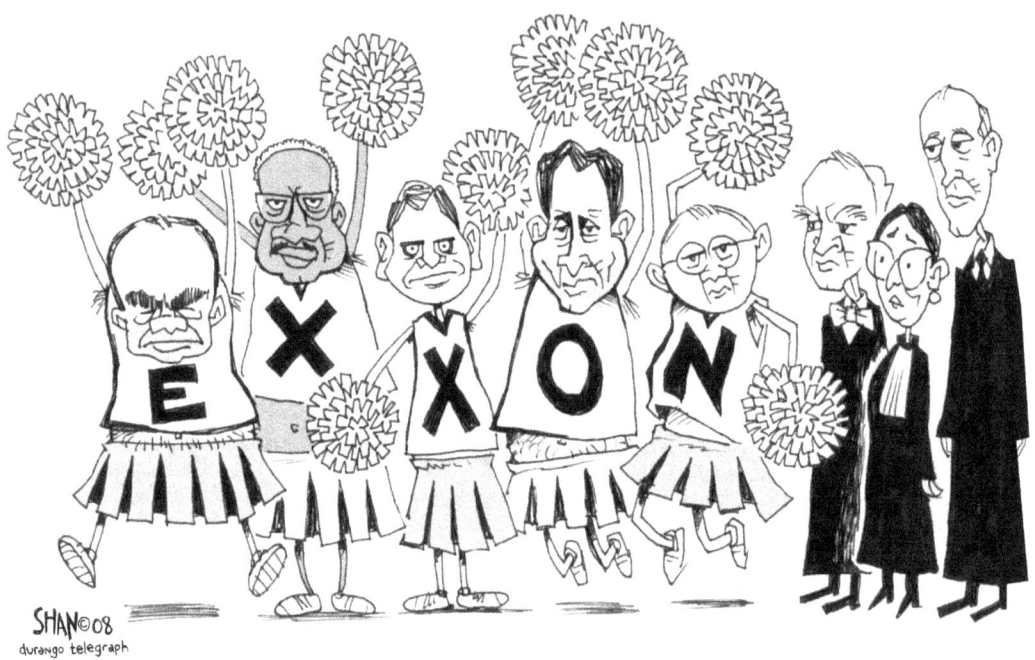

SEE IF YOU CAN FIND THE **ACTIVIST JUDGES** ON THE SUPREME COURT:

SHAN©08
durango telegraph

In 1989, the Exxon owned oil supertanker *Exxon Valdez* ran around in Prince William Sound along the west coast of Alaska. The resulting wreck spilled 750,000 barrels of crude oil into the pristine waters of the Sound, causing immense damage to the natural and economic ecology of the region.

Naturally Exxon was sued, and the judgement was $5 billion against the company in punitive damages. The litigants then entered into a 19 year court battle, which finally ended up in the Supreme Court.

Unsurprisingly, the court split more or less down ideological lines in ruling for Exxon, and reduced the judgement to $507 million.

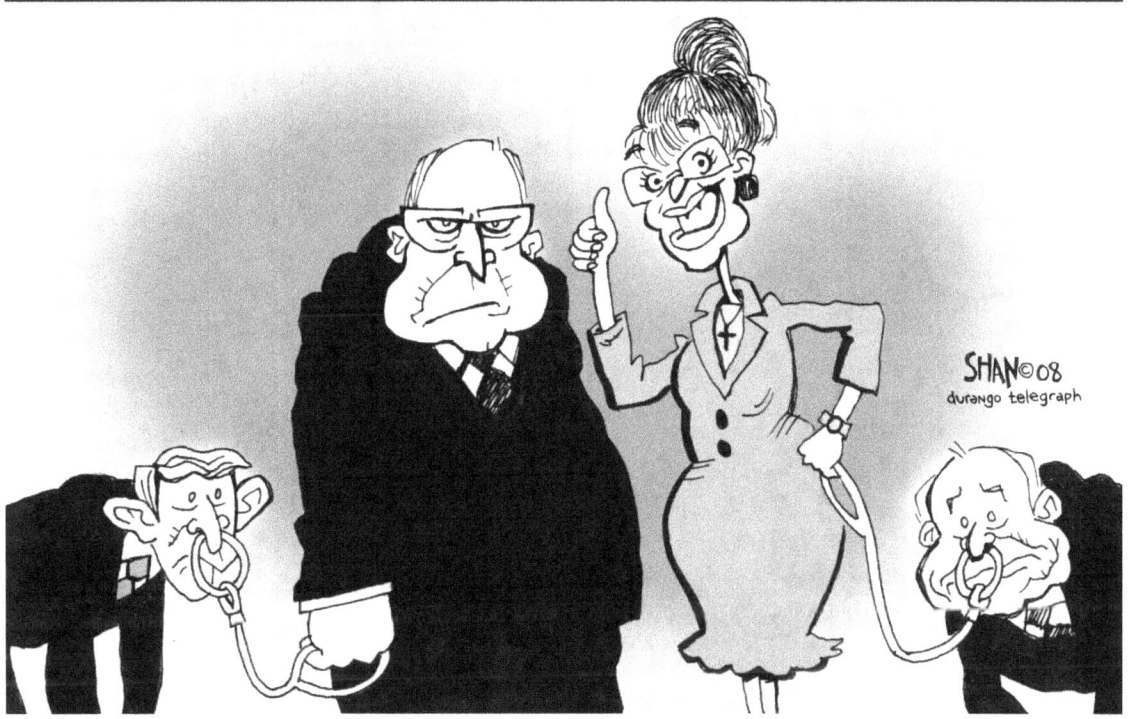

Vice President Dick Cheney was infamous for being asked to find G.W. Bush a running mate in 2000, only to put himself forward as the best choice. It can be argued that Bush's war in Iraq was a direct result of policies Cheney championed over his long life in politics, and there's no doubt that he played a huge role in defining the presidency of a remarkable unqualified "43."

John McCain's choice of Alaskan Governor Sarah Palin to be his running mate in 2008 was initially a cynical choice to subvert and underline Barack Obama's triumph over Hillary Clinton, but quickly devolved into a competition between the two GOP luminaries for the spotlight. Palin won that battle easily, often increasing the turnout for McCain's speeches. As the campaign came to a close, it became clear that she was the favorite of the party base, not the "maverick" from Arizona.

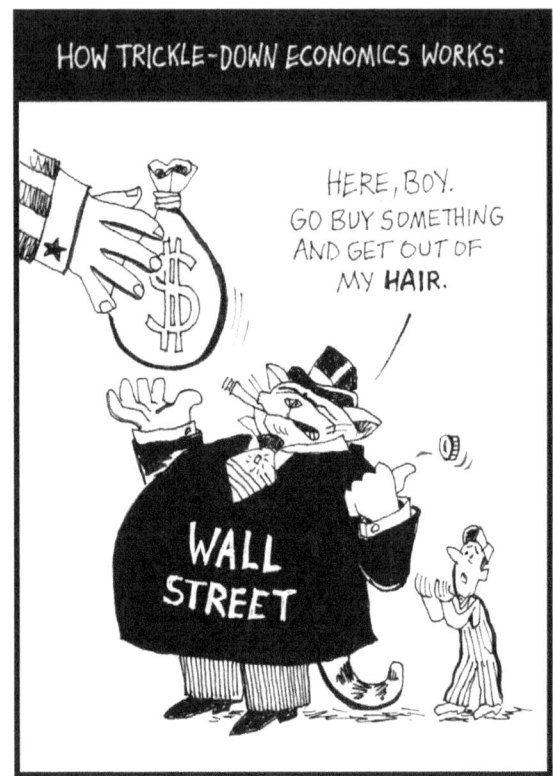
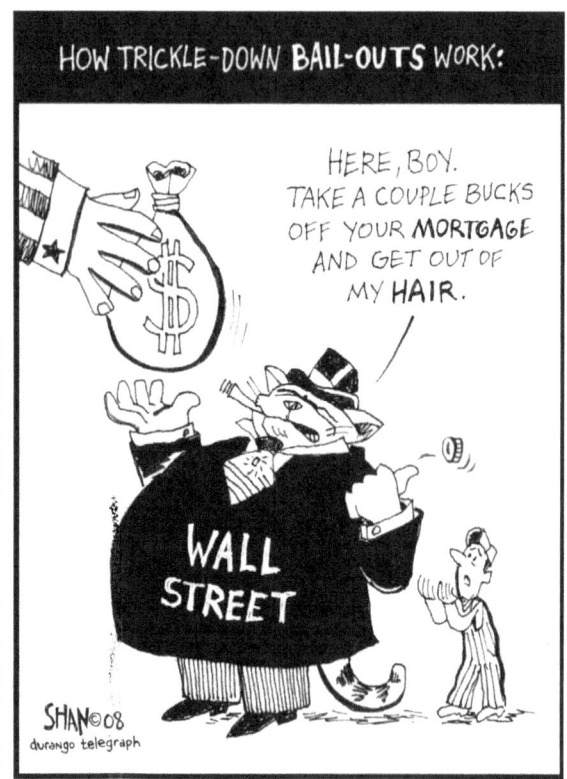

As the 2008 mortgage meltdown began, it was clear that the banks needed to be bailed out or they would fail, leading to a great depression and worldwide turmoil. Bush sent around $700 billion down the rabbit hole and succeeded in stopping the collapse. In return, the bankers whined about being scapegoated, tried their best to stop real financial reform, and refused to lend money out for the sake of the economy they destroyed.

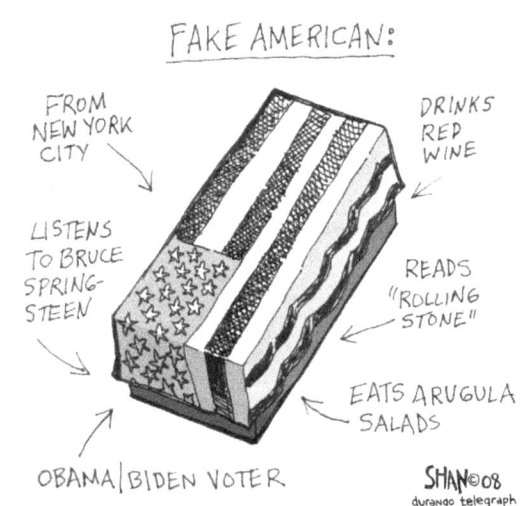

HOW TO TELL REAL AMERICANS

FROM THEM DAMN ANTI-AMERICAN SHARE-THE-WEALTH SOCIALISTS!

REAL AMERICANS

FROM A SMALL TOWN

DRINKS BUDWISER

LISTENS TO HANK WILLIAMS JR.

READS "HOT ROD" MAGAZINE

EATS CHILI-CHEESE-BURGERS

McCAIN/PALIN VOTER

FAKE AMERICAN:

FROM NEW YORK CITY

DRINKS RED WINE

LISTENS TO BRUCE SPRINGSTEEN

READS "ROLLING STONE"

EATS ARUGULA SALADS

OBAMA/BIDEN VOTER

SHAN©08
durango telegraph

THIS PATRIOTIC PUBLIC SERVICE BROUGHT TO YOU BY GUV. SARAH PALIN & REP. M. BACHMANN (R-MN)

Sarah Palin and her ideological sister-in-lunacy Minnesota Congresswoman Michelle Bachmann took great pains during the 2008 election to illustrate the difference between those they viewed as "real Americans" vs.. the rest of the country, who I suppose were "fake." By applying their logic to dead soldiers, I hoped to shine a light on the insanity of such reasoning. Unfortunately, all this work got me was hate mail for showing a military coffin.

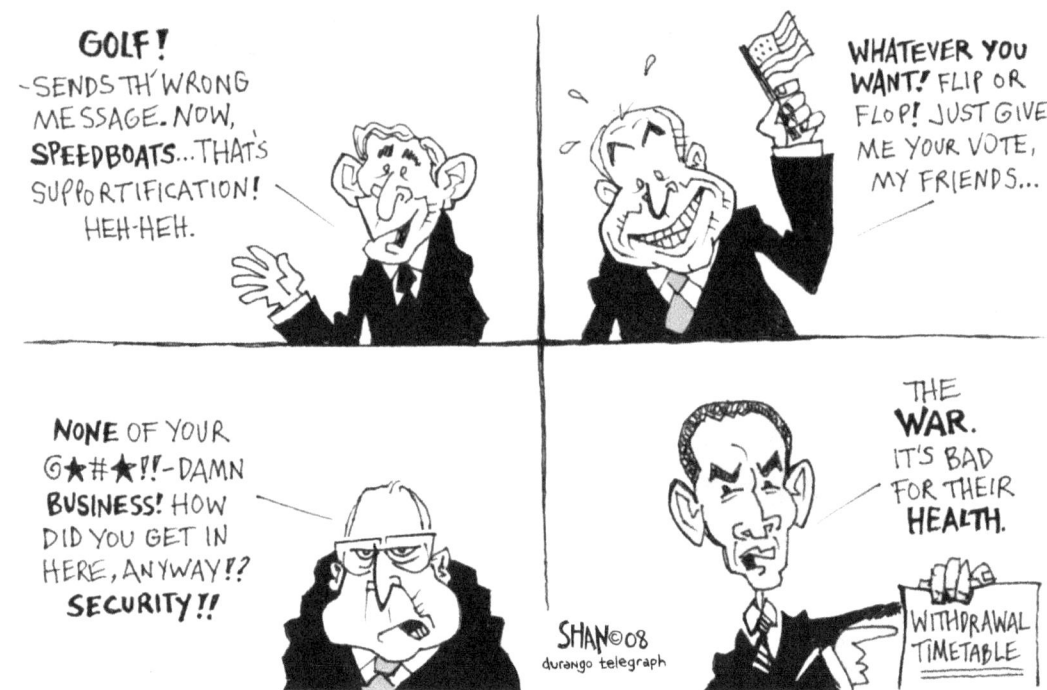

Believe it or not, Bush claimed in to have given up golf in 2003 to support the troops. Apparently, the August 2003 bombing of the United Nations headquarters in Baghdad made a big impression, and G.W. didn't want to send "the wrong message" to soldiers fighting in an illegal war of neocolonial occupation.

However, Bush had knee problems in 2003, and he played his last round of golf in October of that year, so you can decide for yourself how much sincerity was in the great sacrifice.

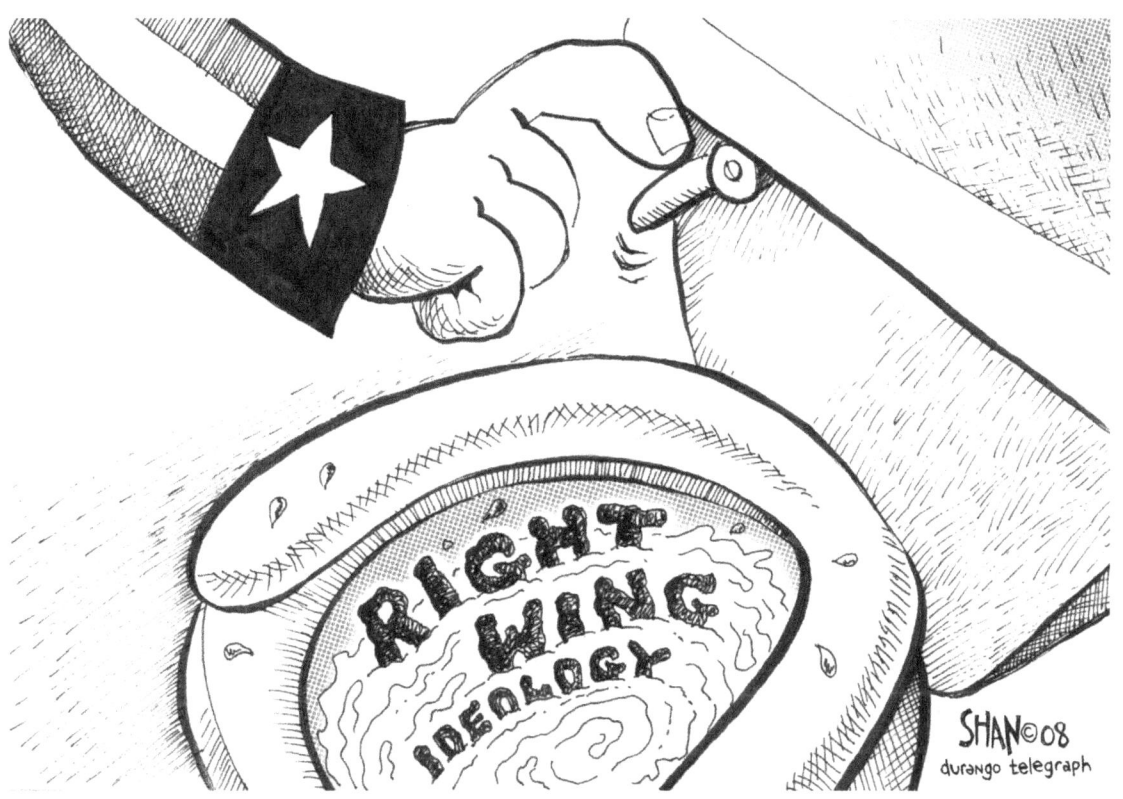

Ah, hindsight. The historic upheaval and landslide of 2008 swept Barack Obama into office also swept a majority of Democratic Governorships, state house, local boards and commissions...it seemed that the world really was about to change. Looking back on this cartoon from the vantage point of 2010, it seems that the demise of right wing ideology was greatly exaggerated.

However, we still have two years to go...

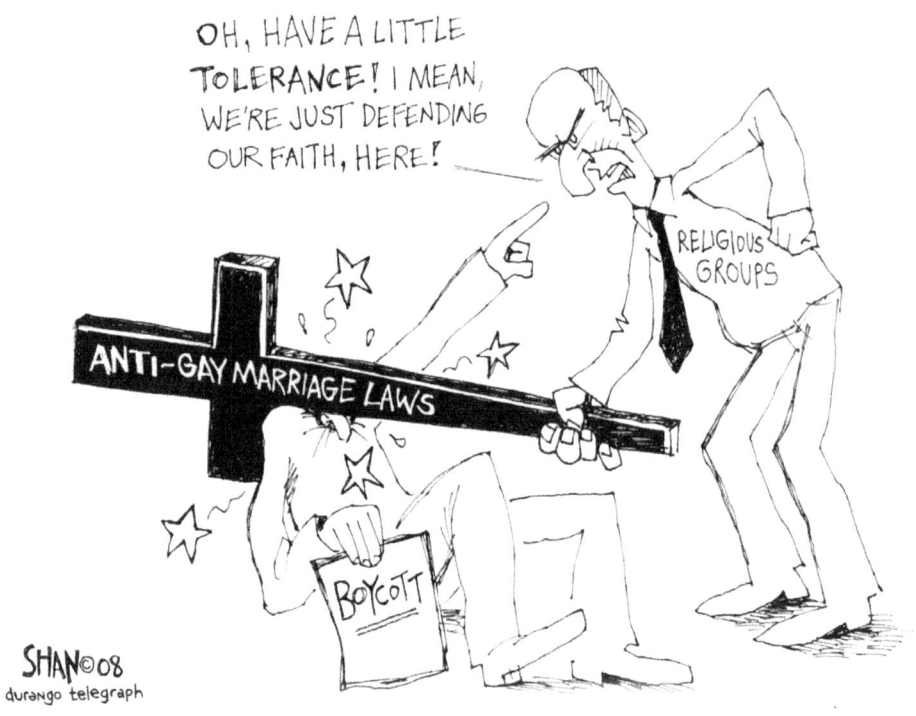

California withdrew the gay marriage right granted by its courts via a ballot proposition, about the only thing that the right was able to accomplish in 2008. After the election, it became known that the Mormon Church in Utah had played a large role in pushing Prop 8. This lead to a large boycott of the state as well as several Mormon-owned businesses.

The 2010 Supreme Court decision of *Citizens United* made it much easier to lobby without responsibility, as nonprofit groups can now give without having to identify their donors, so boycotts may well become a thing of the past.

This cartoon sparked the usual backlash of regressives upset that I should be intolerant of their intolerance. The irony sometimes makes my head spin.

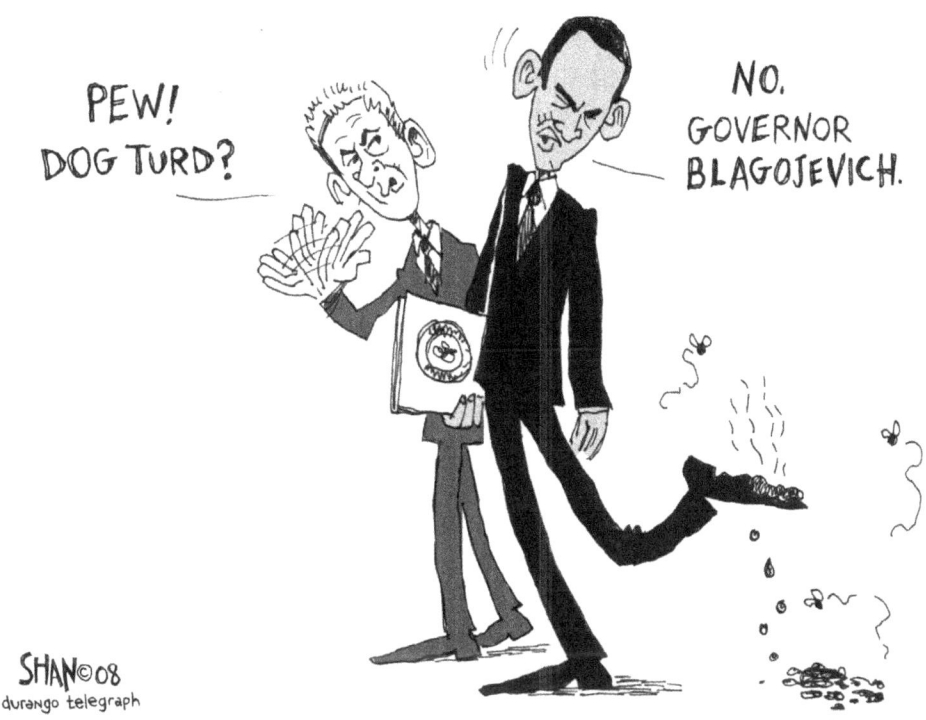

Barack Obama's Senate seat was vacated when the Senator from Chicago left to become President, and Illinois Governor Rod Blagojevich, (bla-goy-o-vitch), moved to fill it by seeing who would pay him the most. Fortunately, he was caught on tape doing this, and was removed from office as a result.

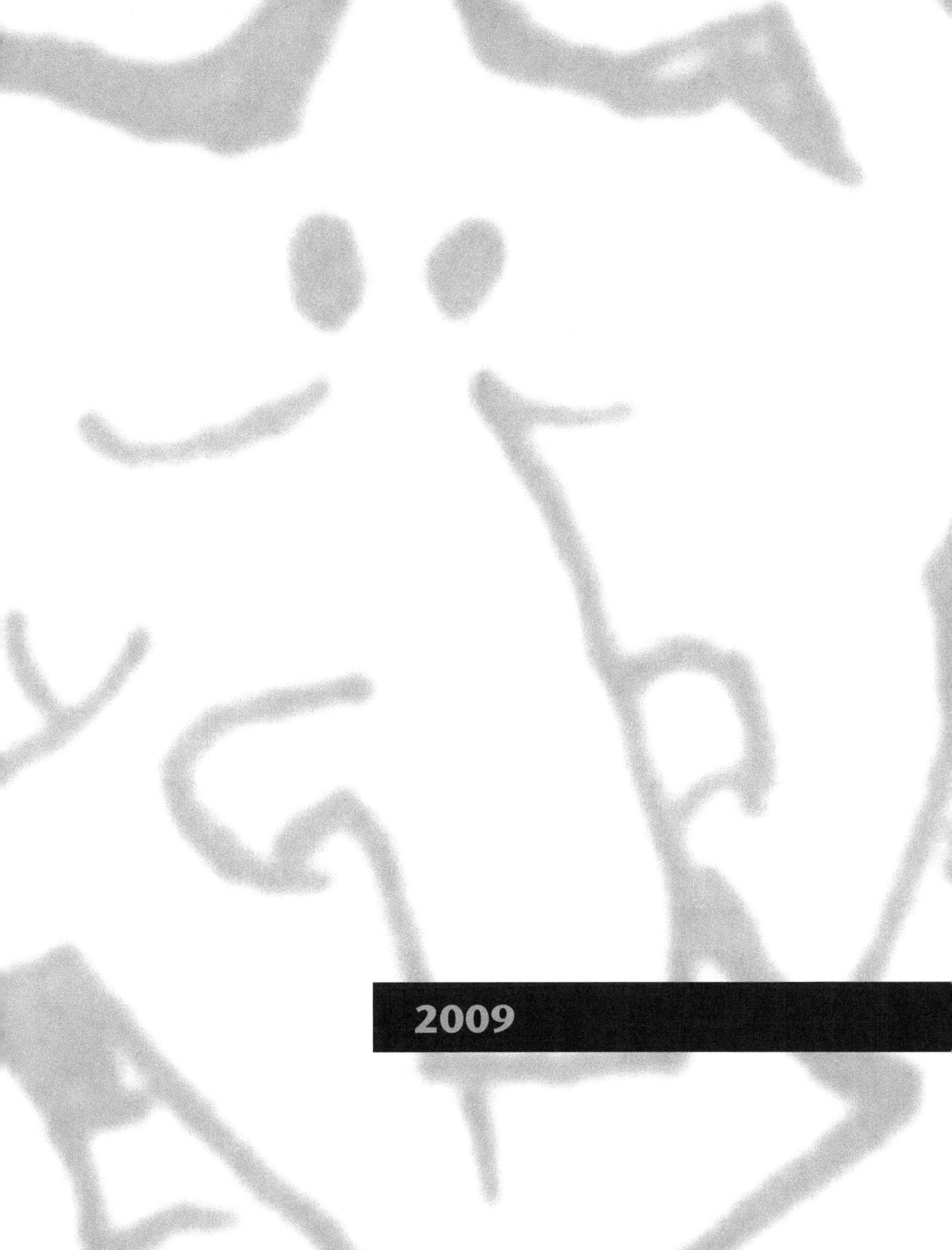
2009

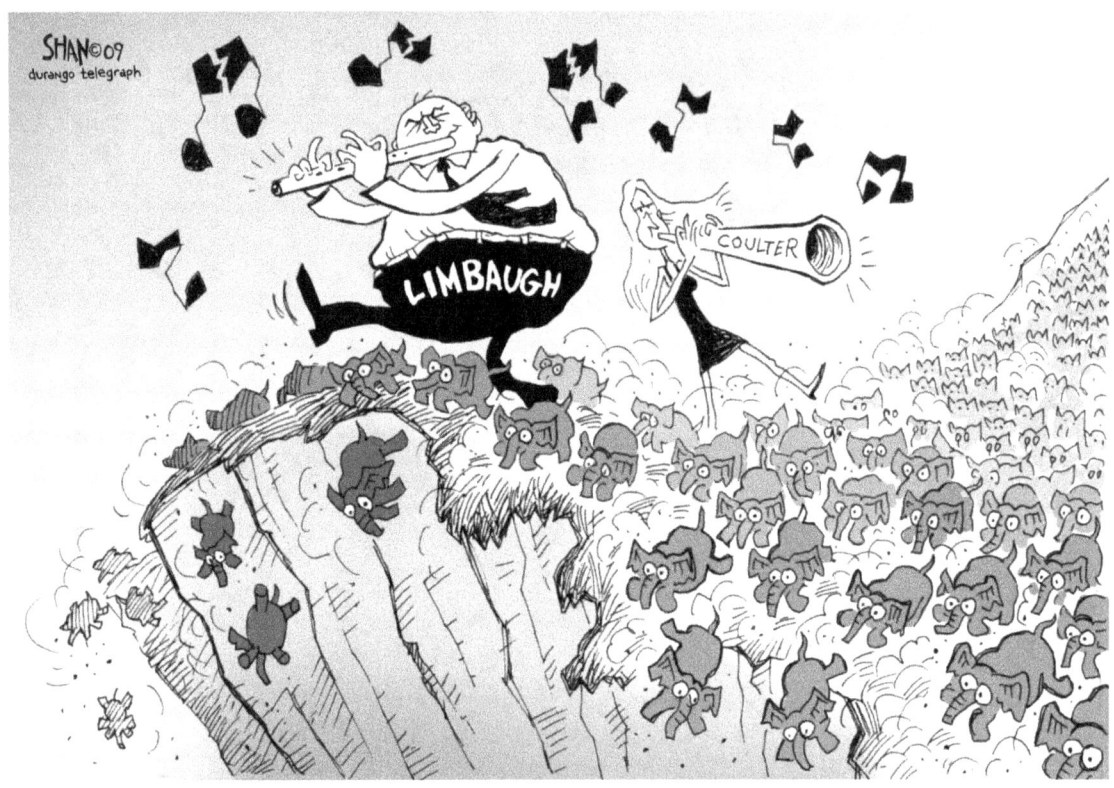

I had a love/hate relationship with I Love Lucy when I was a kid. I was embarrassed for her and the situations she'd get herself into. Watching the 2009 slide of the GOP in to nutballdom was similar - I was cringing, but fascinated and highly entertained.

That fascination quickly turned to horror when I realized around halfway thought the year that the poison being served up by these folks was a delicacy of rare order to the Tea Party people. However, I felt confident that the American people would reject such rare batshit nonsense as death panels and Hitler comparisons.

The 2010 mid-terms proved me completely wrong. It was not elephants the pundits of the hateful right were luring off a cliff, but independents. Perhaps we could use Dodo birds as their symbol.

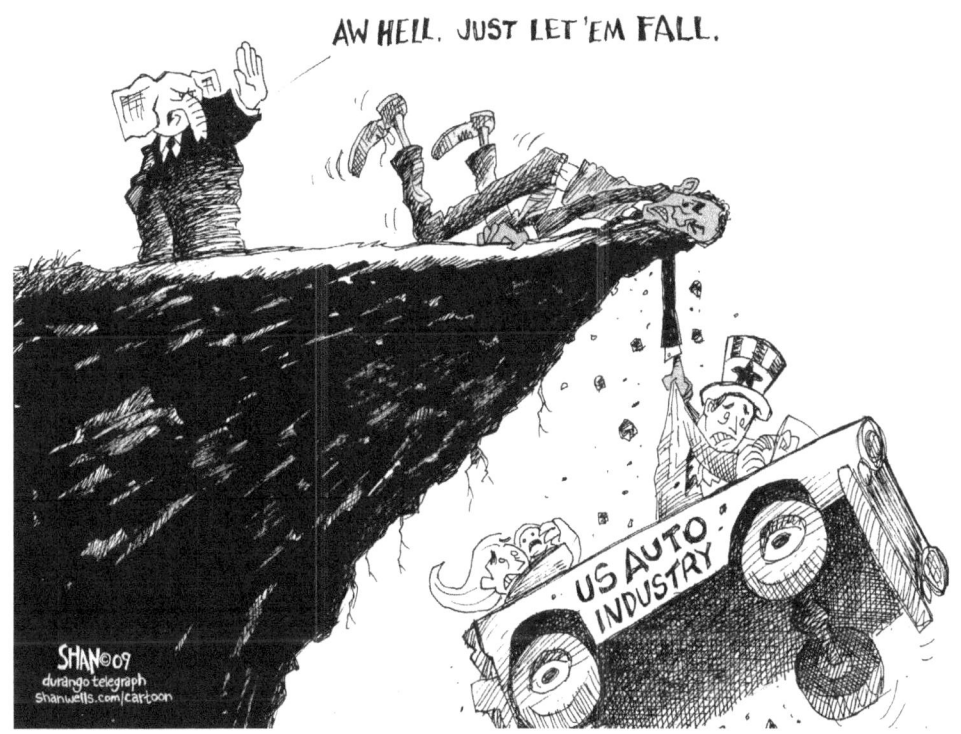

The US auto industry tanked during 2008 along with rest of the country, ad threatened to take down a huge portion of our economy with it. Regressives, already pissed off that the banks had not been allowed to fail and start another depression, now screamed about the government taking over private businesses as Obama moved to prop up GM. Ultimately, GM declared bankruptcy and moved slowly back into profitability, allowing the govt.. to sell off it's interest.

No doubt the shareholders and executives of GM will be forever donors to the Democratic Party for help given in a time of great need. Uh-huh.

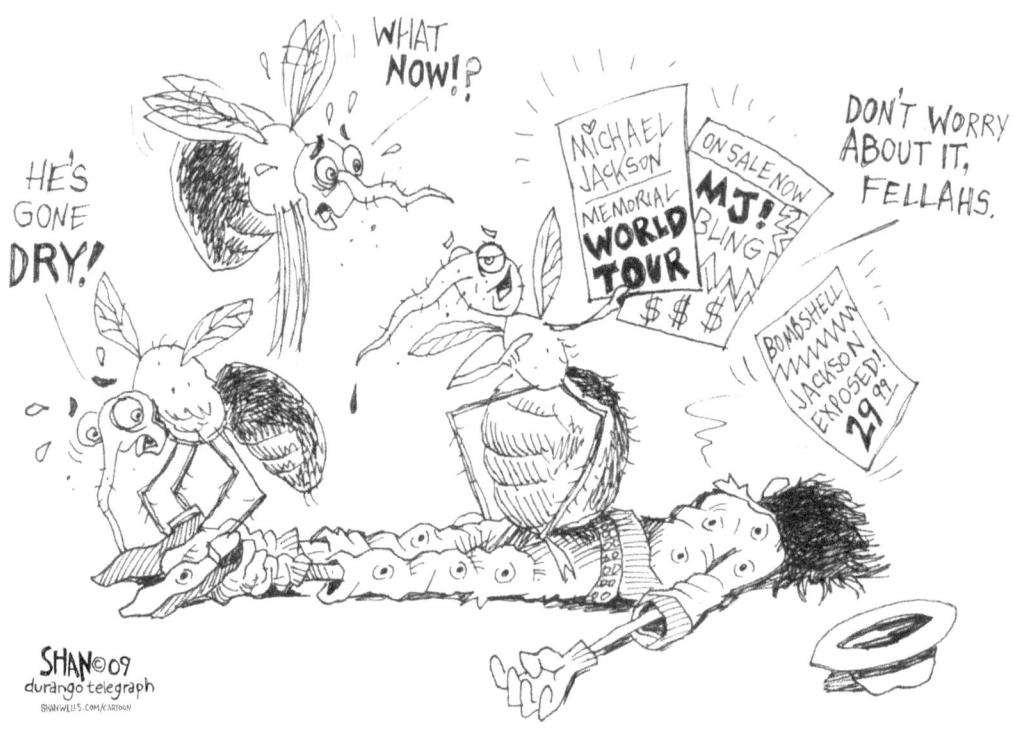

I was a fair Michael Jackson fan back in the early 80's, but lost interest as my tastes matured. The accusations of child molestation he weathered were nasty, and I always had the feeling he was just able to buy his way out of the mess he had created. There was no doubt at all he was a very strange dude. But then, growing up in showbiz has to blow some pretty big holes in your personality.

The singer died in 2009, apparently accidentally poisoned by his doctor. I was moved by the retrospective of his life and works, *This is It*, which was released posthumously in the same year. The documentary captured, above all else, a consummate performer who at age 50 could still out-move the teen dancers hired for his concert tour, and could roll out a flawless, funky bass line using only his voice.

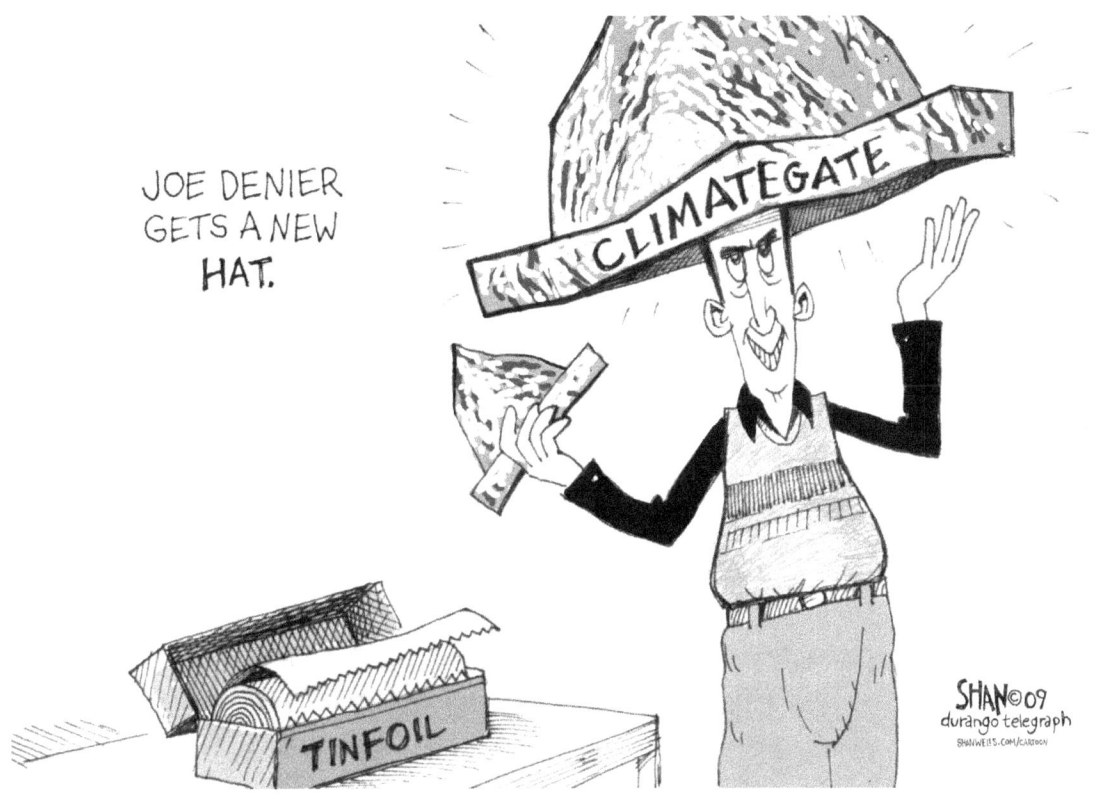

JOE DENIER GETS A NEW HAT.

CLIMATEGATE

TINFOIL

SHAN©09
durango telegraph
SHANWELLS.COM/CARTOON

In mid-2009, a trove of private e-mails were stolen from the East Anglia University Climate Research Unit, or CRU, and made public to great controversy. Several senior researchers had angrily vented in what they thought was a private forum about climate change deniers that bedeviled them and the problems that arise whilst doing a difficult job. They then very unwisely discussed the possibility of refusing to give data to those same deniers since it would be distorted and used to sow doubt. The resulting brouhaha was called "Climategate."

By the end of the year, every rational person had concluded "Climategate" was a straw man. But a new type of denier had been birthed by the incident, one that we might call a Neo-Luddite. These folks are not content with simply rejecting science. Instead, they work to destroy it. Old school deniers previously attacked specific scientific findings. Neo-Luddites gleefully attack the very institution of science itself, claiming that science is incapable of producing a truthful answer because its institutions are irredeemably corrupt. This tactic opened a particularly nasty Pandora's Box. If climatology can be attacked, why not evolutionary biology, or medical science? Whatever is not wanted can be hounded out.

Driven out of their minds by the mere possibility the 2009 Copenhagen Climate Summit might produce something meaningful, deniers worldwide warped into analogs of William Golding's ship-wrecked schoolboys, worshiping the crudest forms of power and sharpening a stick at both ends for any nasty rationalists who might spoil the party.

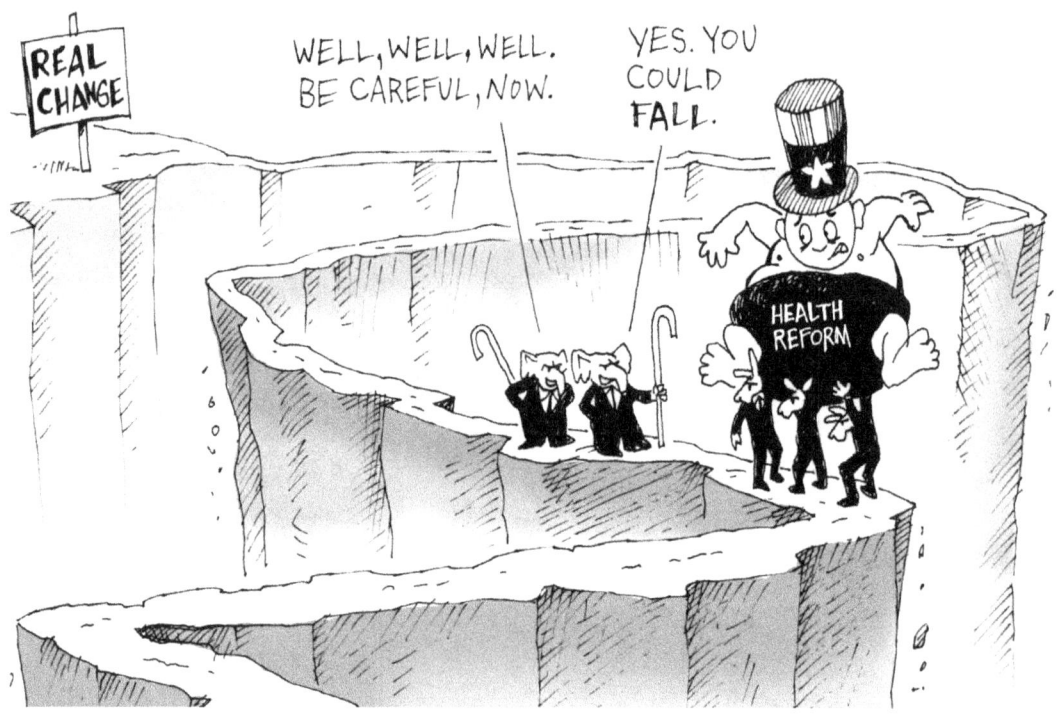

As Democrats moved forward on health care reform, it became abundantly clear that republicans were not about to let their colleagues get anywhere near the goal of affordable, quality care for all Americans.

I was particularly pleased with this cartoon, as it was a rare instance of drawing, concept, and execution all lining up for a successful image.

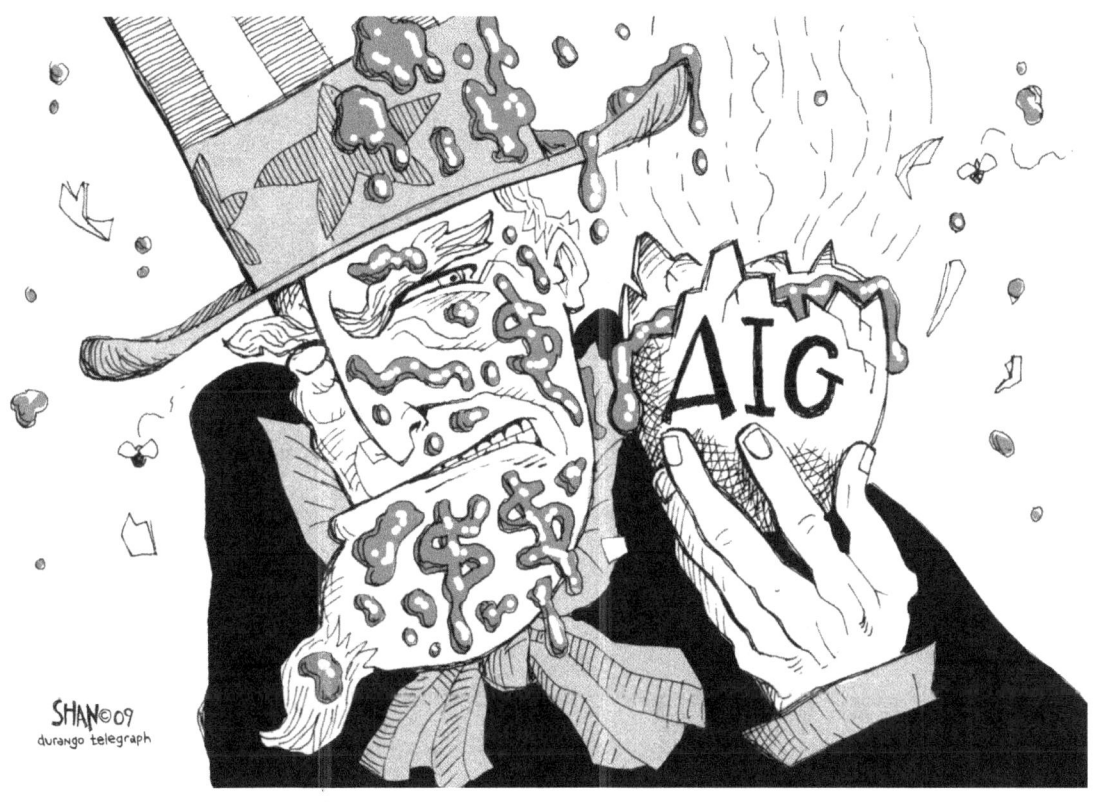

SHAN©09
durango telegraph

AIG, or American International Group, was a major beneficiary of TARP funds as it sank into chaos in the wake of the mortgage meltdown of 2008. The Feds delivered $170 billion to the struggling company to keep it afloat, only to find that over $165 million in bonuses was paid out to the top executives of the company *out of the public cash.*

Despite outrage from Obama and Congress, no banking executive has yet gone to trial, a factor that I feel played strongly in the GOP upset of 2010.

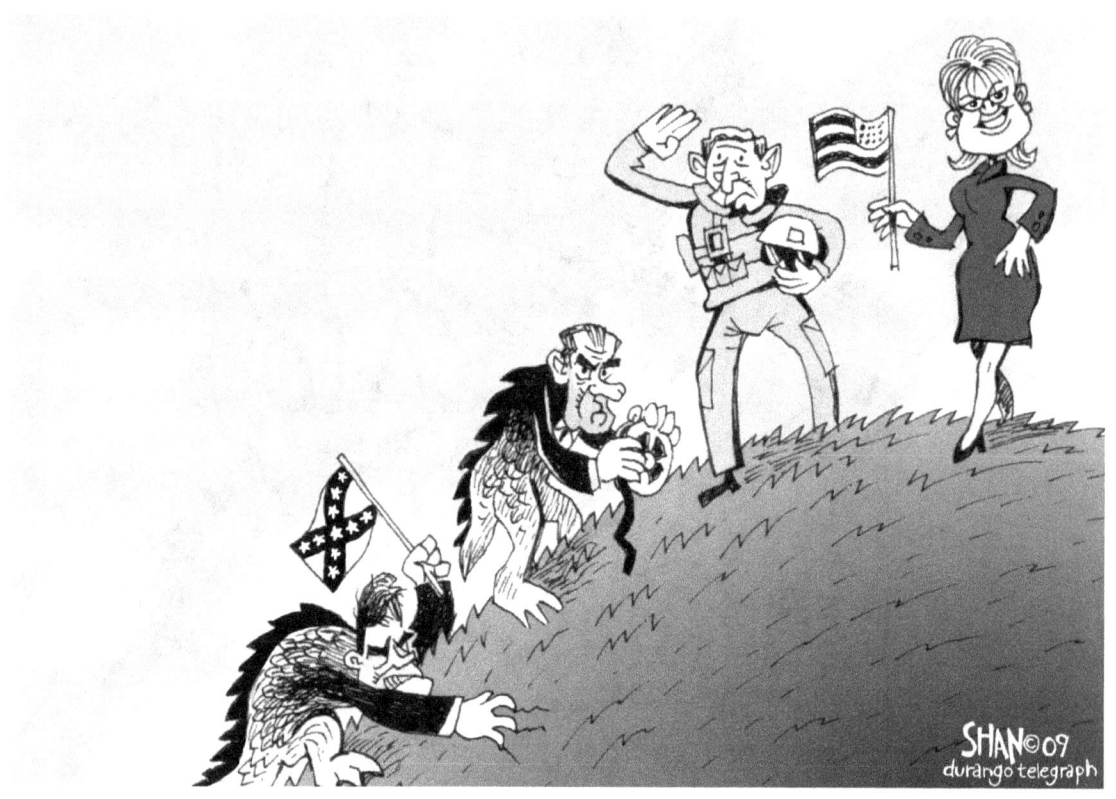

Through dint of her obvious dimness, Sarah Palin is spectacularly unqualified to be President. But that particular attribute may not be the thing that decides if she's going to try for the Oval. In fact, it may not be important at all.

Bush was not qualified to be president either. A "C" student with no particular passion for much other than coke and booze, W. spent most of the first half of his life doing the rich dick thing and embarrassing his parents. However, George did have one shining attribute. He was a charismatic.

W. succeeded because he was the perfect puppet for men who lacked the charismatic presence that is the only true necessity in these times of tweets and sound bites. Using Bush as a proxy, orcish neocons like Cheney were able to advance a radicalized version of American Exceptionalism that was previously relegated, literally, to the crazies.

Sarah Palin could easily be the newest species in a highly successful linage of such proxies. Groomed to be passionate about her righteousness, she wraps herself shallow glamour while being perceived by a frighteningly large number of Americans as "genuine." Palin is Bush 2.0. She represents a new level, the next step in a political evolution that is increasingly convinced that only a rigid ideology of short-term exploitation and control will solve humanity's problems.

In fact, she's perfect for the job.

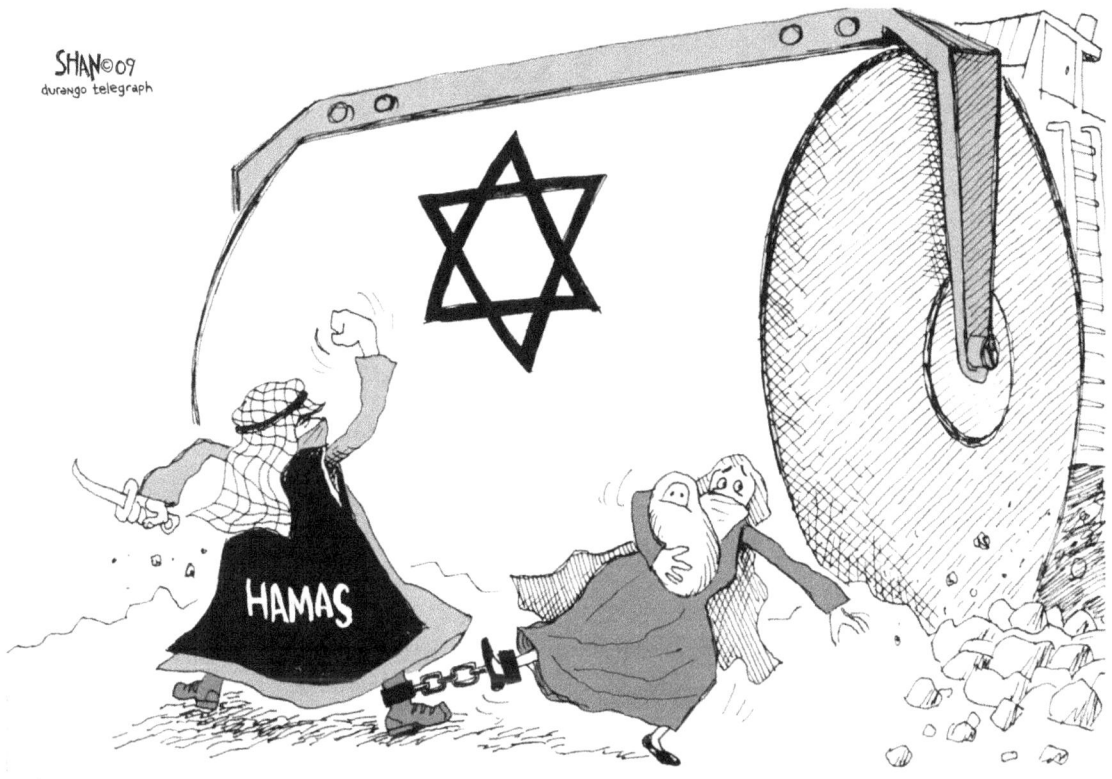

I usually get hate mail about my Mid-East cartoons. This one provoked praise, I suppose because it shows an woman chained to her man, and that says something about the way women are treated in parts of the Islamic world. And that, in turn, speaks to the rather sick proclivity of some resistance factions to set up shop in areas densely populated by civilian non-combatants.

Yet, I was pleased with this cartoon because it tells more than one story, and that's the kind of complexity I aim for but seldom achieve.

As bad as Hamas is in subjecting it's vulnerable populations to harm, the state of Israel has few compunctions about steamrollering those same innocents, despite it's claims to the contrary.

Editorial cartooning, for me, is about more than a simple regurgitation of popular opinion in visual form. At its best, the art form can reveal a deeper truth about issues that seem on the surface to be black and white.

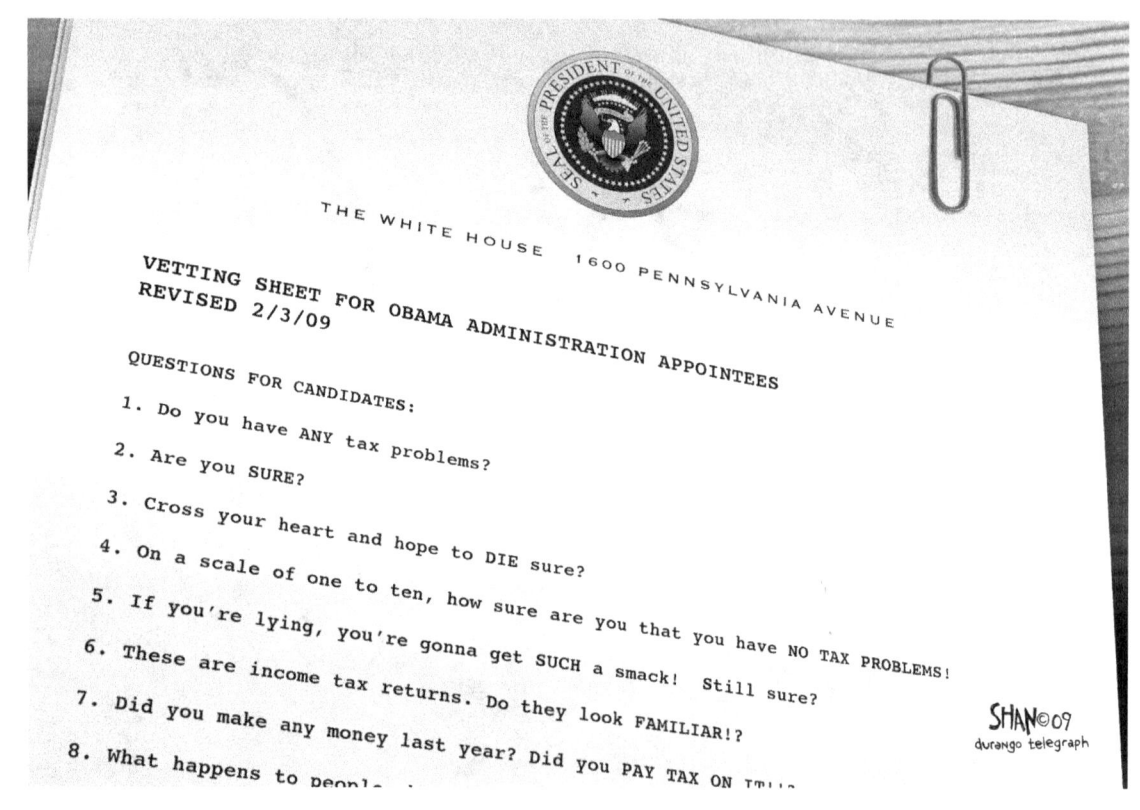

THE WHITE HOUSE 1600 PENNSYLVANIA AVENUE

VETTING SHEET FOR OBAMA ADMINISTRATION APPOINTEES
REVISED 2/3/09

QUESTIONS FOR CANDIDATES:

1. Do you have ANY tax problems?

2. Are you SURE?

3. Cross your heart and hope to DIE sure?

4. On a scale of one to ten, how sure are you that you have NO TAX PROBLEMS!

5. If you're lying, you're gonna get SUCH a smack! Still sure?

6. These are income tax returns. Do they look FAMILIAR!?

7. Did you make any money last year? Did you PAY TAX ON IT!?

8. What happens to people . .

SHAN©09
durango telegraph

As the Obama Administration ramped up and began filling posts high and low, a disturbing trend started to appear.

Tom Daschle, a former Senate majority Leader was tagged for having late paid around $120,000 in back taxes. Bill Richardson, the then Governor of New Mexico, likewise withdrew himself from consideration for Commerce Secretary due to a state contracting investigation.

Nancy Killefer, chosen by President Obama to be the chief White House performance officer, in charge of scrutinizing government spending as a deputy at the Office of Management and Budget, also pulled out because of a tax related issue.

What is it about the high and powerful not paying their fair share?

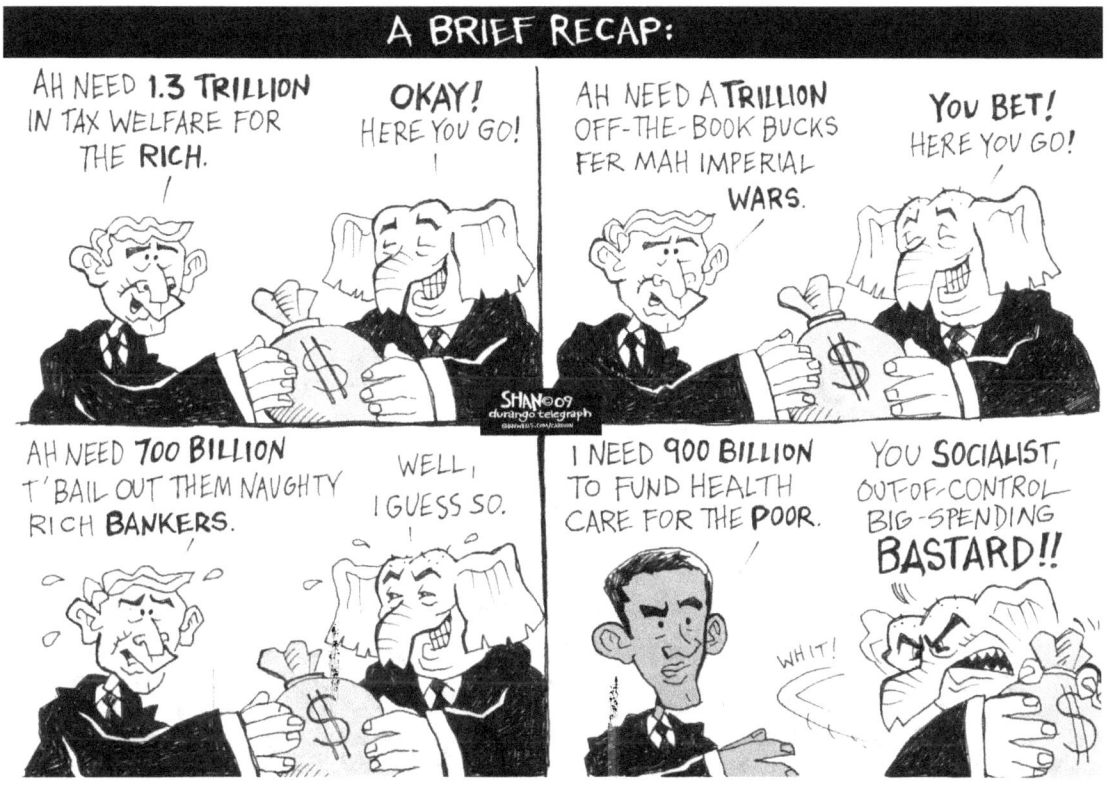

I tried many times to make this cartoon. It was important to me to show how insanely disingenuous the Republicans were in 2009-2010. With this version, I finally made the grade. Often times it's a simple comparison, rather than any convoluted concept that is best. It's deeply troubling to me that Americans have such a poor memory that they will believe any nonsense dished up, as long as their wallet is concerned.

Job growth and debt reduction have long been much better under Democratic Administrations than under Republicans. A quick run down of just the jobs statistic is illustrative:

Richard M. Nixon (Republican): increase of 2.16 percent a year
Gerald R. Ford (Republican): increase of 0.86 percent a year
Jimmy Carter (Democrat): increase of 3.45 percent a year
Ronald Reagan (Republican): increase of 2.46 percent a year
George H.W. Bush (Republican): increase of 0.40 percent a year
Bill Clinton (Democrat): increase of 2.86 percent a year
George W. Bush (Republican): increase of 0.01 percent a year

While there are some caveats to these figures, the overall trend is clear: Democrats averaged 2.03 annual job growth, compared to 1.07 for Republicans. And yet the Republicans are seen somehow the party of growth.

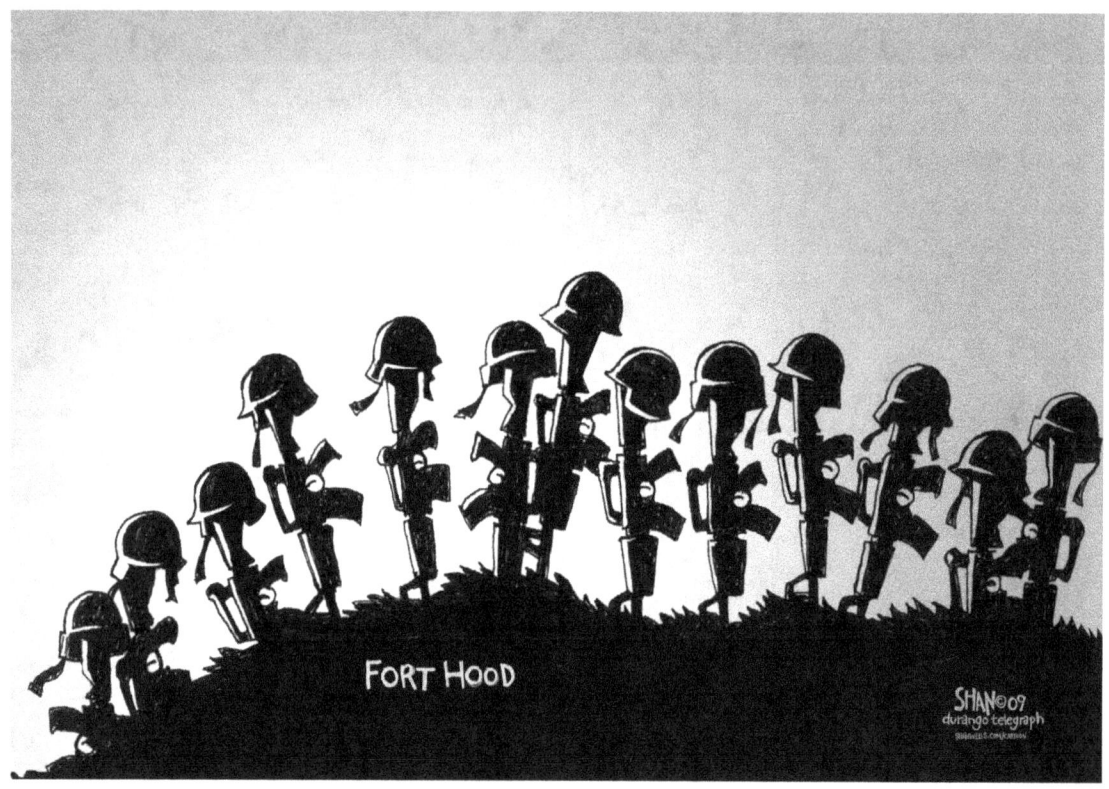

Nidal Malik Hasan, a U.S. Army major serving as a psychiatrist at Fort Hood, Texas, blew a fuse an began a shooting rampage on November 5th that left 13 soldiers and one civilian dead. At the time I did this cartoon, it was assumed that the 13th victim was a soldier. I regret not knowing the real story so that I might have made a better memorial.

As with Columbine and Red Lake massacres, there's little to say about such tragedies, other than to try and find an image that conveys a sense of loss and remembrance.

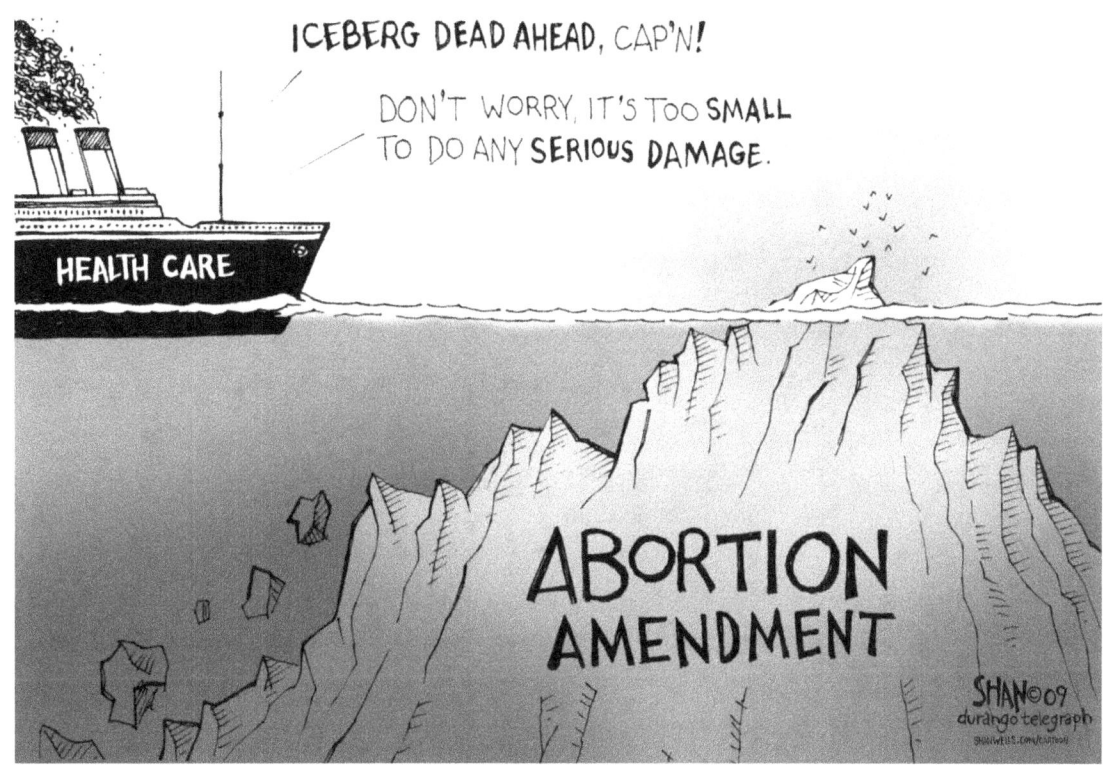

As the Dems steered their precarious way towards passage of real health care reform, a very nasty bit of politicking got in the way. Bart Stupak, a Michigan Senator and one of the bluest blue dog Dems, refused to pass the Senate approved health care reform bill without an amendment prohibiting the payment of abortion services with federal funds under the new law. Stupak assembled a tight little cadre of like-minded blue dogs, and went to the White House to make a deal.

Obama promised to outlaw the use of federal money with a executive order, and the crisis passed, but not without a few held breaths from those of us who actually wanted and approved of the bill.

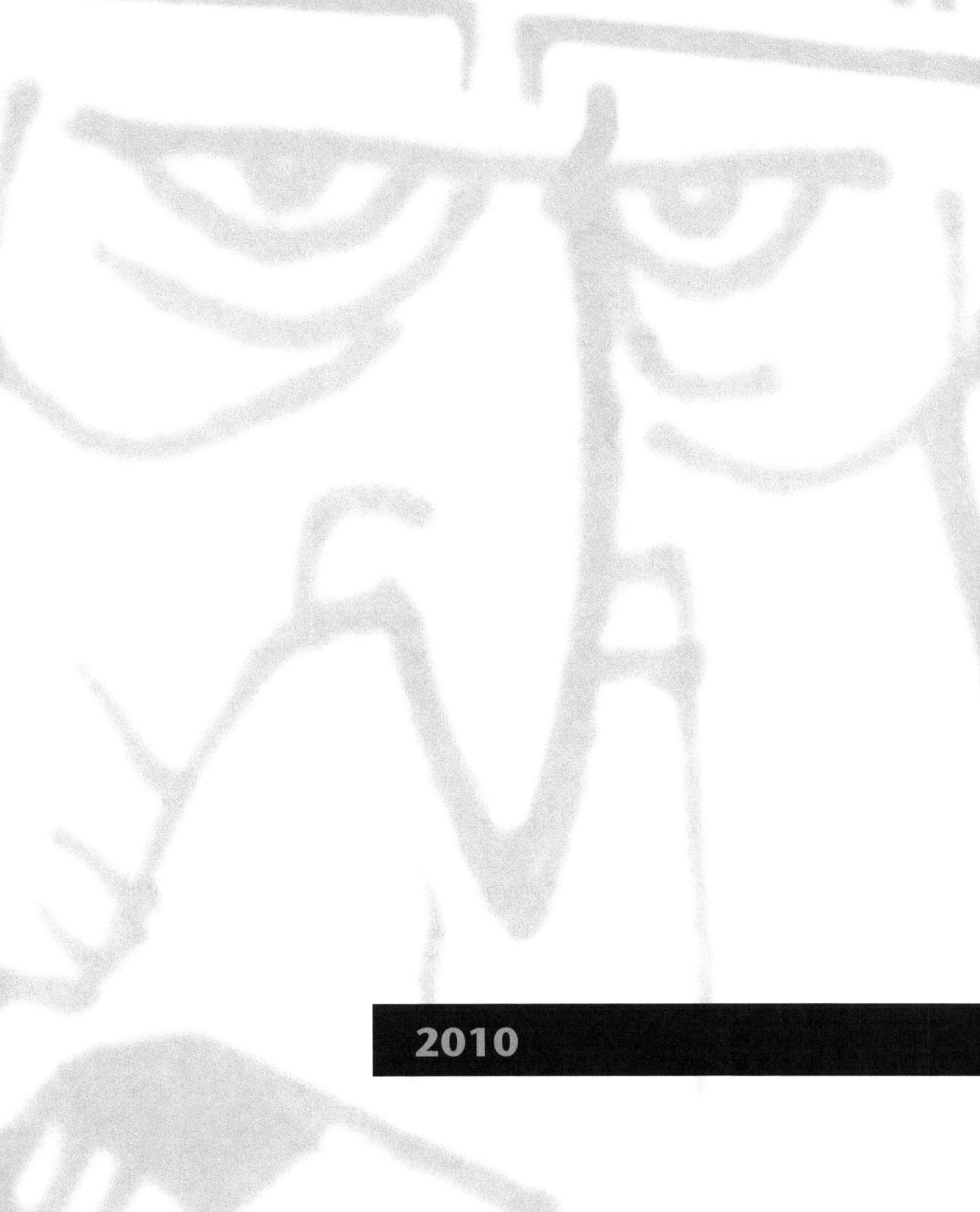

2010

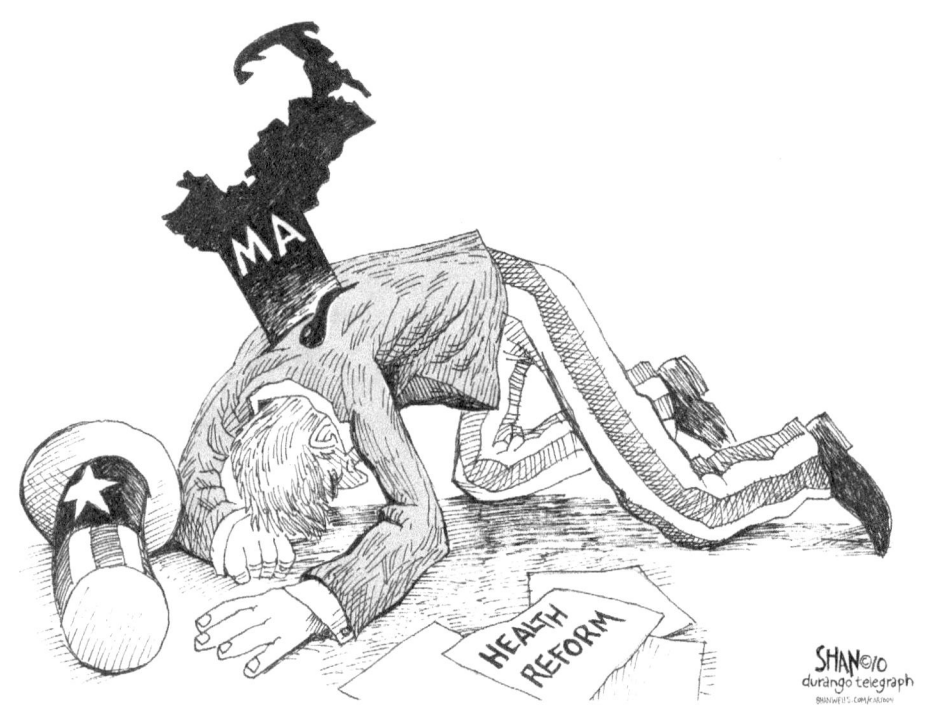

Every Thursday I have coffee with a good friend whose politics are opposite mine. We tend to look for common ground, and here's one patch we agree on: America is starting to look ungovernable. As pundit Steven Flynn put it: "the U.S. has become like a bus where everyone has a brake. It won't run."

Senator Ted Kennedy's death in 2009 prompted a special election in Massachusetts for his open seat. In a harbinger of the 2010 midterm "shellacking," the Obama Administration only twigged to the fact that the seat was at risk for GOP conversion late in the game, and so could do nothing to stop it from going to a Palin understudy, Scott Brown. This took away the tenuous 60 vote super majority enjoyed by Dems in the Senate, and complicated health care reform tremendously.

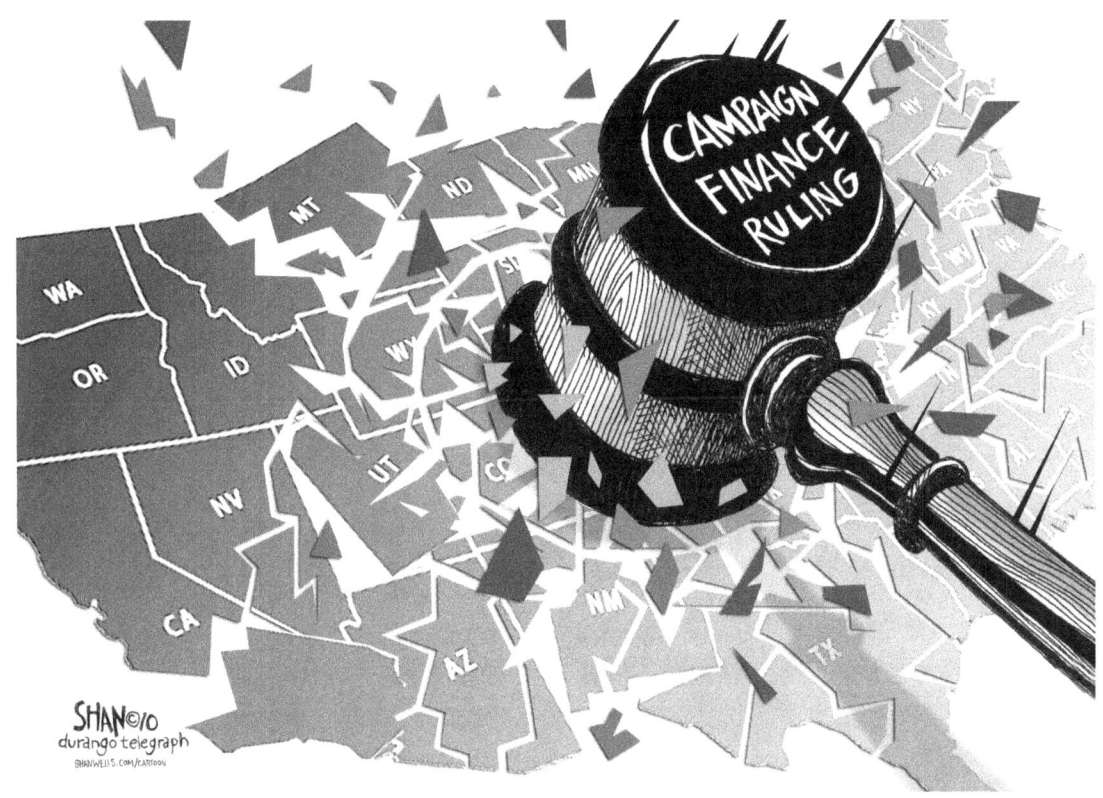

G.W. Inc. let loose the Dogs of War to chew Iraq to pieces. With their ridiculous ruling on Citizens United vs. Federal Election Commission, the Supreme Court, (or at least the stupid members of it), loosed the Pigs of Corruption, shattering 80 years of steady effort to keep big money from buying the country. Not that the law ever did a great deal of disinfecting, but at least it shown a dim light on the country's bribe bosses.

Of course, the logical progression of this nonsense was for a corporation to run for office. After all, they are seen as persons in the eyes of the law. With the ruling, they were granted the right to speech. Why not go whole hog and ditch the formalities?

That particular joke occurred to the Progressive PR Firm Murray Hill. These fine folks protested the ruling by running for the House as a corporation in Maryland's 8th District. Murray Hill Inc.'s campaign video received more than 220,000 views on YouTube. Although the corporation lost, they intend to run again in 2012.

It's pretty funny now, but there is a slight risk underlying the mirth. What if they win?

Exxon for Senator. Coca-Cola for Speaker. Wal-Mart for President. God Bless America.

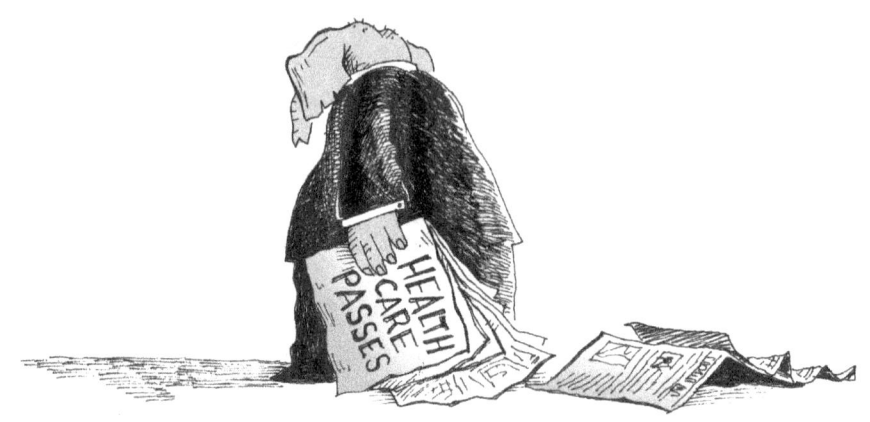

THREE THINGS FOR REPUBLICANS TO REMEMBER:

1. IT'S **NOT** THE END OF THE WORLD.
2. IT'S **REALLY NOT** THE END OF THE WORLD.
3. WE STILL NEED YOUR VOICE. DON'T DISENGAGE.

SHAN©10
durango telegraph

After months of wrangling and setbacks, Democrats were finally able to pass historic health care reform in 2010. Not single payer, not perfect by any means, but a pretty damn good start. And, of course, there was an immediate backlash. Republicans in the form of a grumpy John McCain put the country on notice that everything and anything the Dems do would be stonewalled because... well, because they won.

I didn't begrudge the GOP a little bitterness. The ones that weren't totally in the pocket of the insurance cabal actually seemed quite sincere in their ideology. The utter despair I saw amongst their ranks reminds me of how I felt when Bush went to war. I could relate to that hollowness of the chest, and the almost constant stress headache.

I disagree profoundly with the conservatives, but I don't want a war. I want them to have a voice, a seat at the table. I want that because I continue to hope that they might see, when the earth does not go screaming into the sun over the next few years, that progressives actually have some pretty good ideas. And, I want to know what they think, too, because they are Americans who deserve to be heard.

Unfortunately the GOP reaction to Health Care passage was to double down on the crazy, winning the House in the Mid-terms and ensuring gridlocked government until 2012.

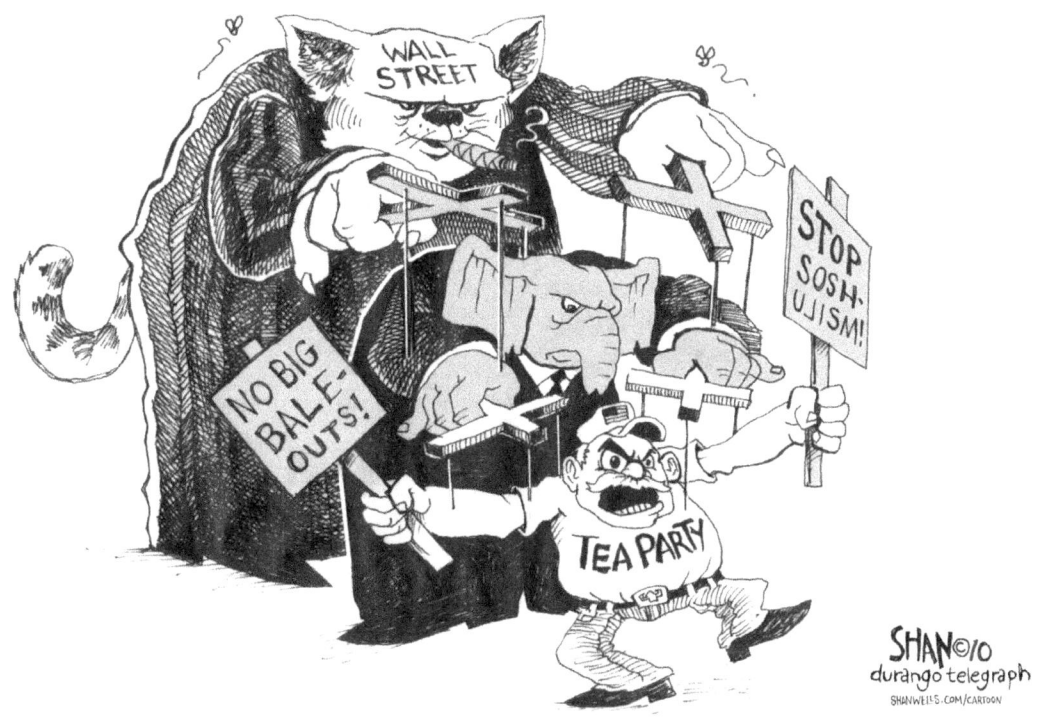

The battle over banking regulations in 2010 had every bit of the nutty gasbagging witnessed in 2009 as the health care debate raged. That bit of nastiness brought us the Tea Party, which was quickly seized on by Republicans as their ticket back to the big leagues.

Financed by shady multi-billionaires like the Koch Brothers, the Tea Party managed to advocate the positions of the ultra rich, while calling those fighting for reforms that would benefit the elderly and poor among us, (who make up the vast majority of the Tea Party movement), elitists.

The proclivity to fight passionately against one's own best interests had never seen a more pure manifestation than those poor puppets who spent the summer of 2010 waving misspelled signs and ranting about socialism.

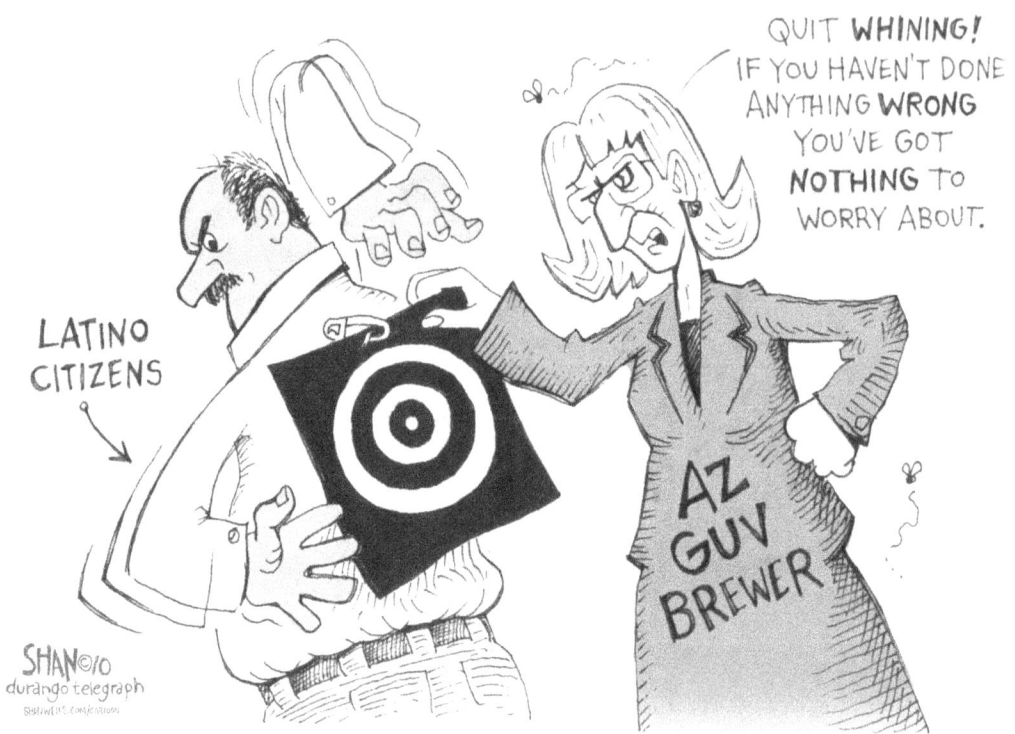

Arizona's GOP made huge mistake with their panicky blunder into immigration law in 2010. There are pressing problems with that state's border, but the new statute required officers to check the immigration status of those they detain for other offenses, and required immigrants to carry documents proving they are in the country legally.

The law is a Jim Crow throwback targeting legal Hispanic American citizens. If comparing skin color, hair color, eye color, clothing, and accent is not acceptable for identifying potential Mexican illegals because of racial profiling laws, then exactly how are they to be spotted?

Besides the moral hazards SB 1070 created, it's also unconstitutional. States have no power to pass immigration laws because such laws are the sole province of the Feds. Just as states can't have their own foreign policies or enter into treaties, they can't have their own immigration statues either. And it was precisely on these grounds that the Obama administration sued Arizona to prevent the law form being enforced.

Either you are in compliance with Constitutional law, or you are not. There is no grey area here. The bottom line is that if most Mexicans were white, blue-eyed, and blonde haired, the law would never have passed.

White people don't like a target on their back any more than brown people do.

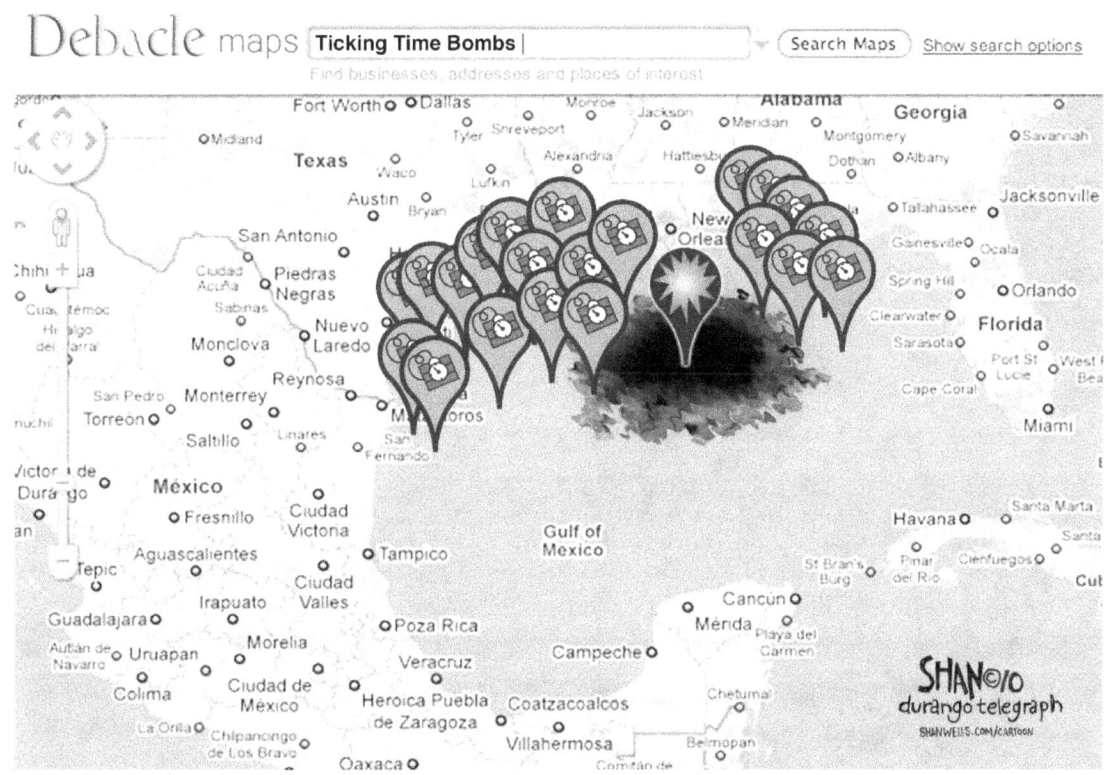

As of 2011, there are 3,858 active oil drilling platforms in the Gulf of Mexico along the southern edges of Texas, Louisiana, Alabama, Mississippi, and Florida.

There is good reason to suspect that other BP rigs may have defective parts and instrumentation. Given that Dick Cheney cheerfully deregulated the bejeezus out of drilling safety laws back in W.'s first term, there's even better reasons to think that all the other platforms may be in a state somewhere between bad and fucked.

Energy is dangerous. Nuclear power coughs up Chernobles. Oil and gas vomit up Deepwater and Valdez size-spills. Coal, our main boy in the energy line-up, is now roundhousing us with global warming. And we just can't seem to get on the alternative bandwagon.

Musing on these facts makes one think of the first energy source we tapped, we poor hominids, shivering in the early African dawn: fire. We thought we mastered it. The prohibitions were easy- don't stick your mitts in. Learn that, and the rest follows- from barbecues, to indoor heating, to moonshots.

But we were delusional. We never learned the real mastery of fire. True control does not mean refraining from burning your hand. It means refraining from burning down the forest.

As the Gulf spill debacle so clearly showed, we really suck at that.

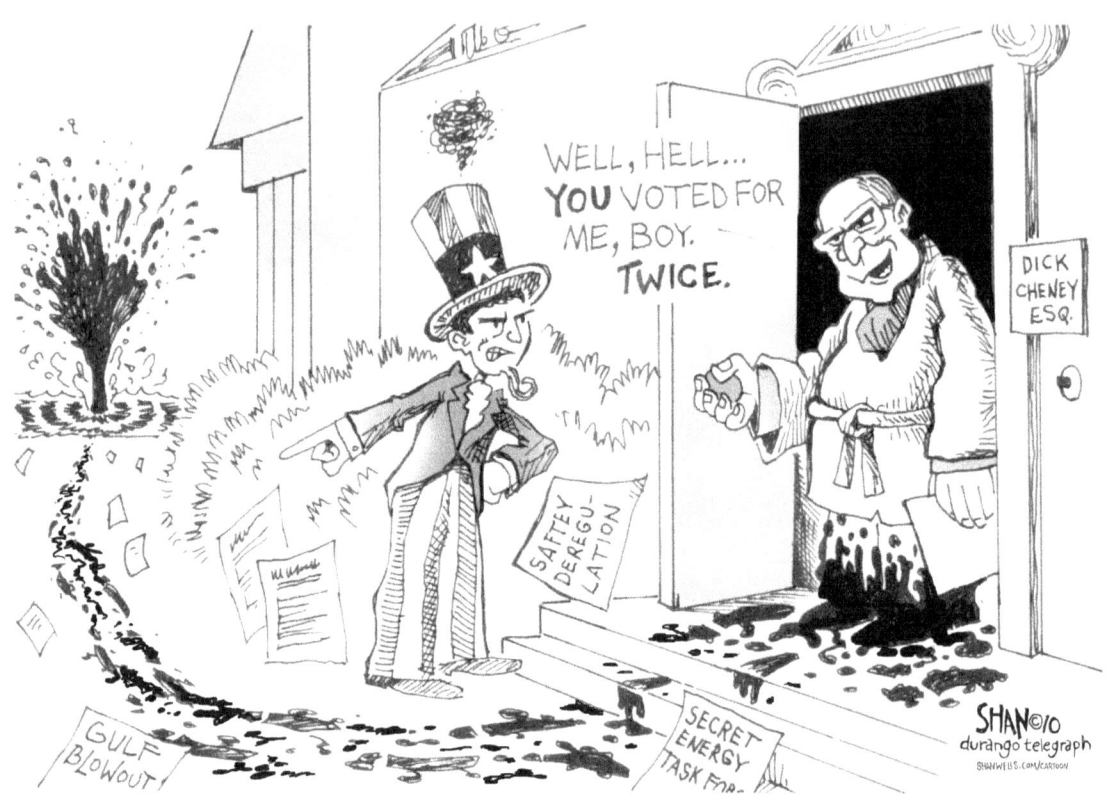

The horrific Gulf Oil spill was blamed on many things, but here is one person at whose feet can be laid the entire disaster, and probably to the surprise of no one paying any attention at all since the year G.W. Bush was appointed, that person would be Dick Cheney.

Robert F. Kennedy Jr., an environmental lawyer and son of the assassinated Senator, traced a clear path of oily footprints straight to the former "co-president" in a *Huffington Post* entry around May of 2010:

> "...between January and March of 2001, incoming Vice President Dick Cheney conducted secret meetings with over 100 oil industry officials allowing them to draft a wish list of industry demands to be implemented by the oil friendly administration. Cheney also used that time to re-staff the Minerals Management Service with oil industry toadies including a cabal of his Wyoming carbon cronies. In 2003, newly reconstituted Minerals Management Service genuflected to the oil cartel by recommending the removal of the proposed requirement for acoustic switches. The Minerals Management Service's 2003 study concluded that "acoustic systems are not recommended because they tend to be very costly."

For some reason, Americans seem to be intolerant of attaching blame for current events to actions by former administrations. It may be a part of our deep cultural desire to always be on the front foot, looking into the future. Or it may just be a deep and malignant societal A.D.D.

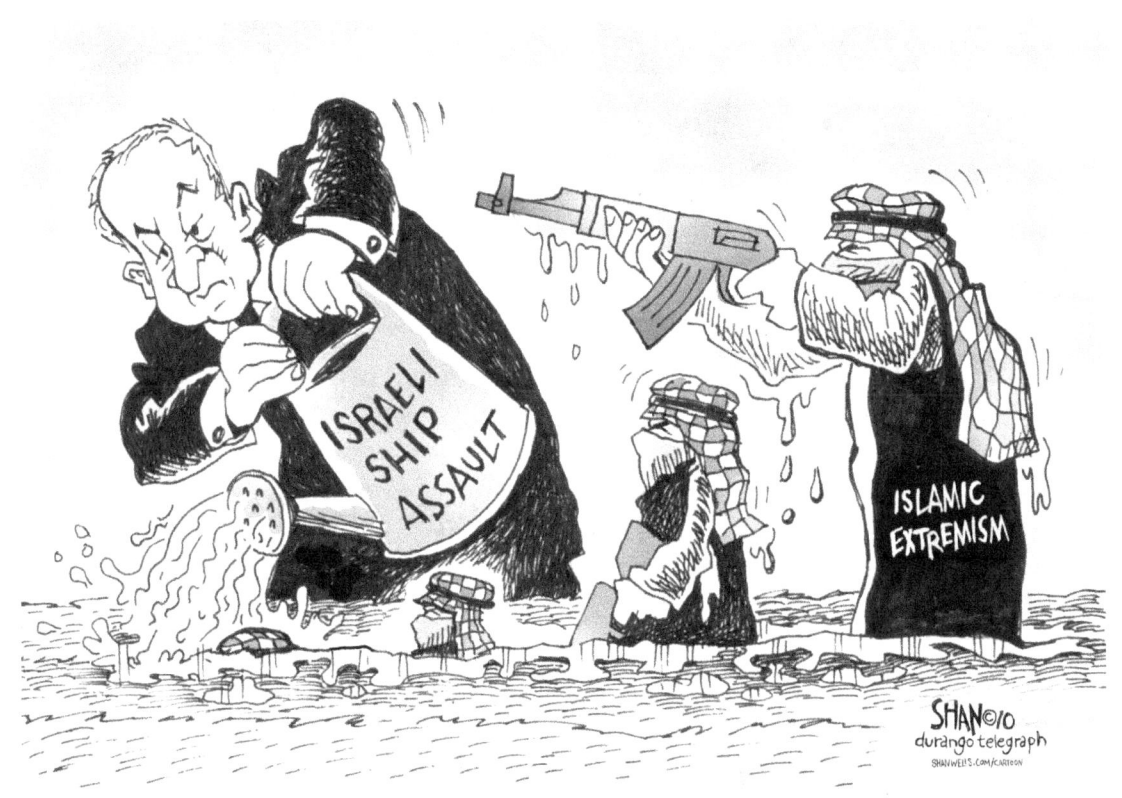

Directly after 9/11, there was a small spurt of sanity regarding the reasons why American had just suffered the worst terror attacks of its short history. Chalmers Johnson wrote an excellent book about it, called *Blowback* that outlined the causes and effects of American Empire.

Sadly, that brief period in which we actually attempted to discern the root causes of terrorism was snuffed out by a tidal wave of groupthink nationalism, engendering classics like "freedom fries" and "they hate us because we're free."

Israel's boneheaded attack on a group of civilian ships carrying aid for Gaza in the summer of 2010 might have been a chapter in Johnson's book illustrating exactly the right way to not only create a new generation of Islamic extremists, but enrage just about everyone else.

Leaving aside the larger question of the blockade's legitimacy, the entire episode could have been handled without drama. Israel could have allowed the boats to dock at Gaza, then distributed the aid or confiscated any alleged weapons without compromising their need determine what was on the ships in the slightest. Instead, in seeming oblivious imitation of the Bush Doctrine, Israel sent heavily armed assault teams abseiling against a group of unarmed activists, including an 18-month-old child, the Irish Nobel peace laureate Mairead Corrigan Maguire, and an elderly Jewish survivor of the Holocaust.

Oy.

THE AUDACITY OF IMPOTENCE

...MY FELLOW AMERICANS...

...FOR YEARS WE'VE TALKED ABOUT ENERGY INDEPENDENCE...

...WE'VE TALKED ABOUT RENEWABLES...

...AND NUCLEAR POWER...

...YES, WE HAVE TALKED ABOUT THESE THINGS FOR YEARS...

...DECADES, EVEN...

...WHY STOP NOW?

THANK YOU, AND GOD BLESS AMERICA.

SHAN©10
durango telegraph
SHANWELS.com/cartoon

When G.W. Bush was elected, those on the rightish side of things were quite happy to relax, knowing that their guy was going to do things well. It was like being on automatic...a cruise control President. And sure enough, Bush didn't disappoint. Taxes were cut, regulations gutted, wars fought, and so on. The conservative banner was being upheld, despite Tea Party claims.

When Obama got the big job, there was some similar hope on the left that he would be our guy, in there fighting the good fight. For the most part, the President has done that, but Obama's non-address regarding the BP Gulf oil spill highlighted some serious problems with "our guy.

The issue is leadership. The hideous black curtain snuffing out life in the Caribbean is only a precursor to the damage climate change will inflict on the world. History handed the President an unprecedented opportunity to grab the wheel of State and spin it. What better than the nation's worst environmental disaster to use as a lever for making bold changes? And yet Obama offered no new legislative proposals, nor described the scope of the problem, or even asked for the American people to do anything except pray.

How pathetic.

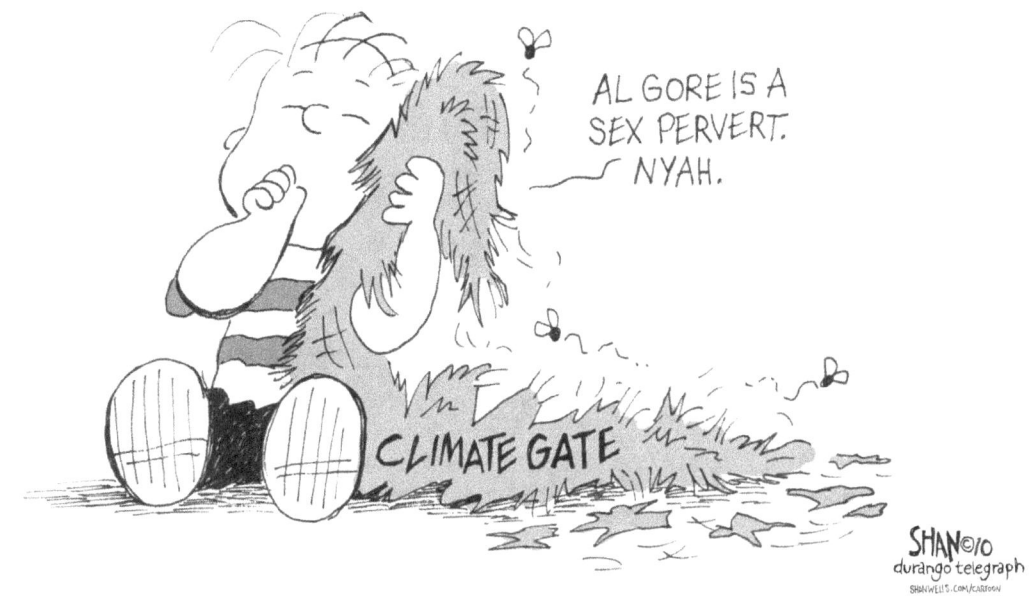

"Climategate" was stroked and milked by the denier community for every cherry-picked strand until it became like a diseased security blanket, held tight in the face of overwhelming evidence and used as a proxy for real analysis. It's hard not to feel personally offended by such willful idiocy.

There is more than enough information from credible, vetted sources that no one should be a climate denier. Yet, there seem to be some that take real pleasure in it. They joyfully name as incompetent charlatans people who have devoted their lives to painstaking research.

I have much more tolerance for skeptics. Climate science is not easy to understand and it's often counter-intuitive. Skeptics at least make an effort. More than that, skepticism is the foundation of science. Questions about how we know what we know have led humanity to golden realms of innovation. It's also led us down some pretty dark alleys, but that's another conversation.

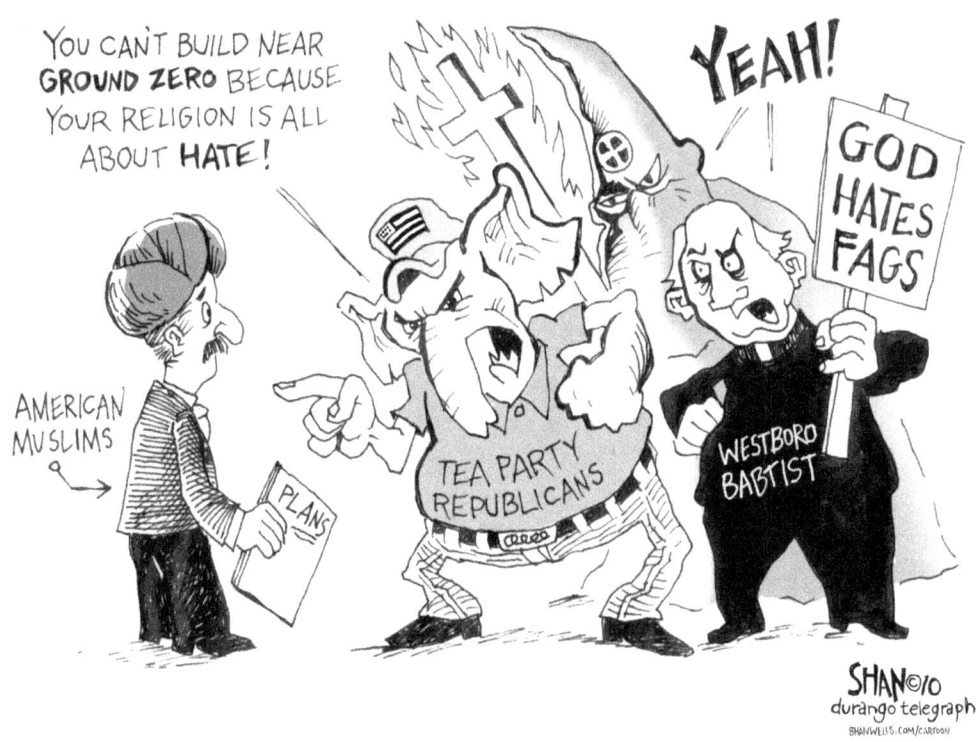

The "Ground Zero Mosque" was not on Ground Zero. It was two blocks away. Nor was it a mosque. It was a community center with a prayer room. Kind of like a chapel in an airport- a place to pray, but not a church, right?

So now that we have the facts straight, we can go on to the utter, shameless, nutballed hypocrisy of the right on this issue. Besides the sheer racism of equating a worldwide faith of millions with terrorism and hate, we could talk about how Westboro Baptist and the KKK are Christian organizations and how absurdly stupid it would be to broadly define Christianity as a hate faith because of them.

We could also address how the Tea Party in particular and Republicans in general have wailed for years now about the sanctity of the Constitution and how inviolate it is. Yet, when confronted with a poster boy issue for First Amendment religious rights, they choose to selectively edit their strict constructionist outrage.

It seems to me that a community center dedicated to multicultural healing, with a 9/11 memorial and a mission of educational outreach, is exactly the sort of thing we would logically want near Ground Zero. But we have gone past logic in the America of Beck, Palin and Gingrich. The melting pot is boiling over these days.

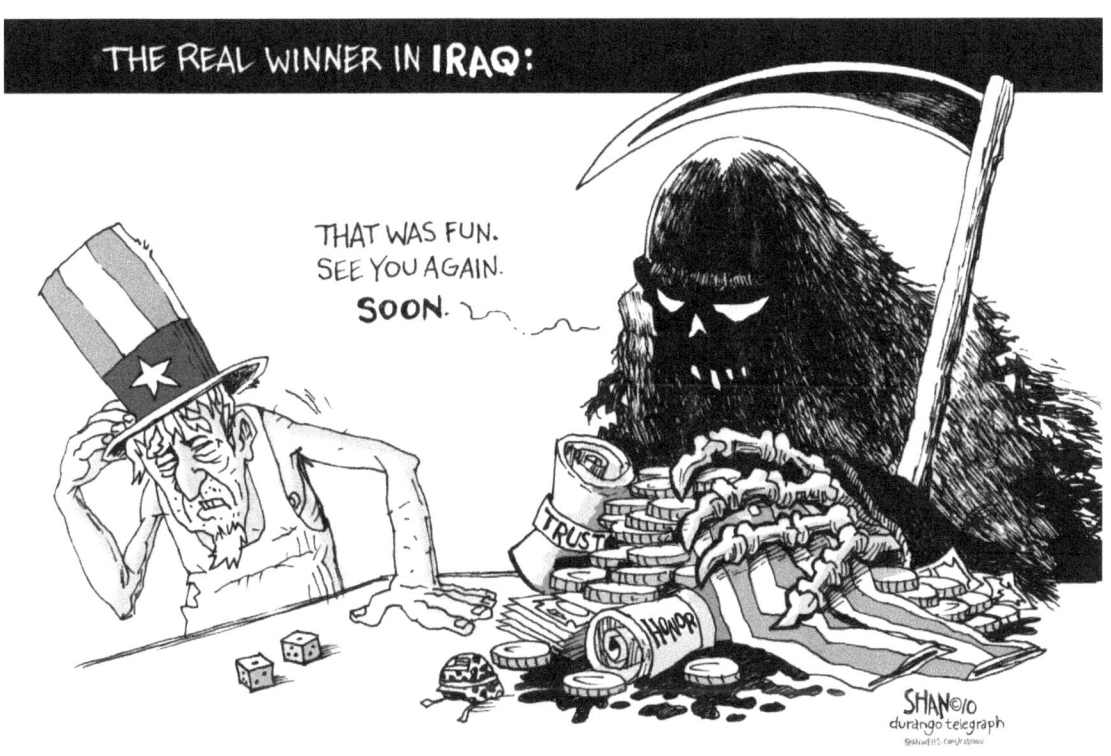

The 2010 pullout of combat troops in Iraq made just about zero news. The country was focused on the economy and seemed to have forgotten just what a complete disaster the war was, preferring instead to debate whether we had "won."

Nothing about the Iraq war is worthy of praise, save the dedication that our soldiers have to the Constitution. Only that dedication could explain the sacrifice they made in the face of the outright lies and pure, naked greed of the Bush Administration. Only that dedication explains why they consented to be brutally exploited, and we as a county should be damn happy that they didn't just overthrow the government out of disgust.

According to *The Lancet*, over 650,000 Iraqis had been killed by 2006, and probably that number is much higher now. Ten years of brutal war and sectarian violence have left the country scarred and deeply divided. US casualties run into the 30,000 range, with over 4,500 dead. Final costs of the war are currently projected at $900 billion, and may well run over $3 trillion.

$3 trillion. Thousands of lives lost. Countries ravaged, and for what? No one has been held responsible, nothing has been gained. And the really scary thing is we seem to have learned nothing from all this, which all but guarantees we will do it again.

There is only one winner here, and it carries a scythe.

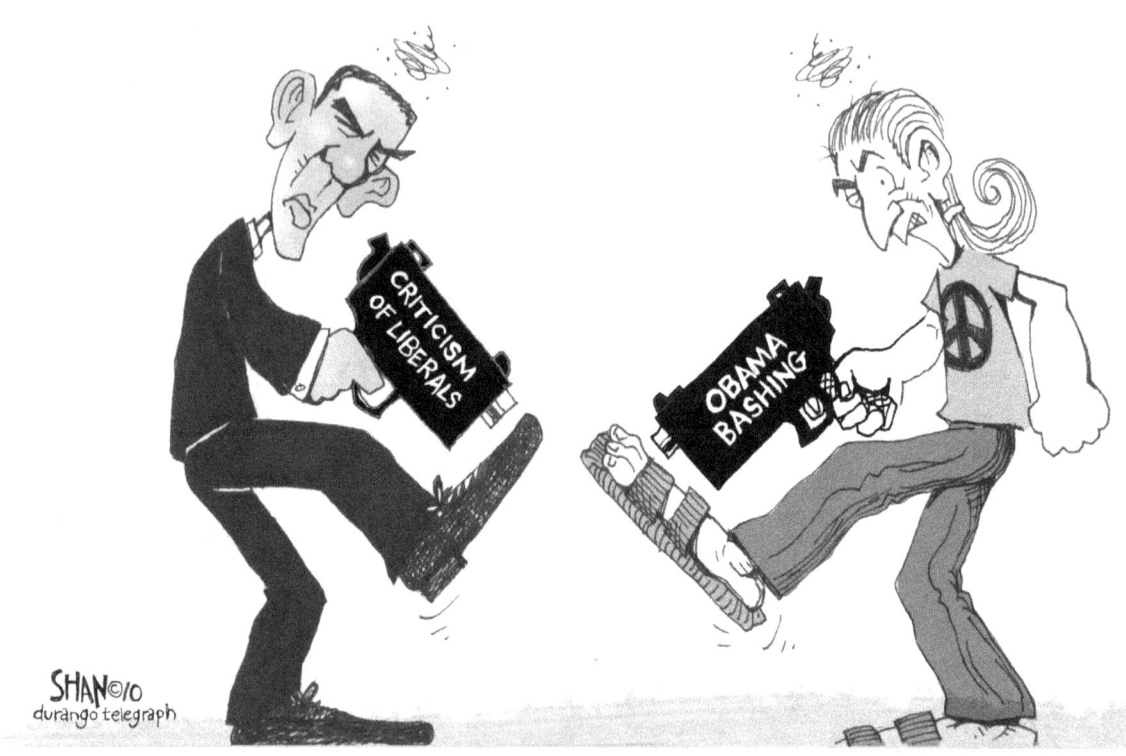

As 2010 played itself inevitably to a dramatic mid-term, one thing became very clear: liberals were unhappy with Obama, and Obama was unhappy right back. From his admonition to "buck up" to VP Biden's infamous whining" remark, the honeymoon was clearly *so* over.

I could relate to liberal discontent. Obama handled the BP oil disaster horribly. His backing away from his own stimulus package to the point of being unable to even use the word was a complete debacle. He came late to the game of campaigning, seemingly focused on governing, unaware he was about to get run over. And his insistence on "bipartisanship" with a GOP that would prefer to be covered in ants before compromising a thing...bordered on the pathological.

However, the President's actual accomplishments when viewed from only a short height, are breathtaking. Few others who have held the office accomplished so much in so short a time, and yet got so little credit for it. Part of the credit for that failure is due to the White House PR people, who apparently spent much of 2009 asleep, but there was a creeping racism at work as well.

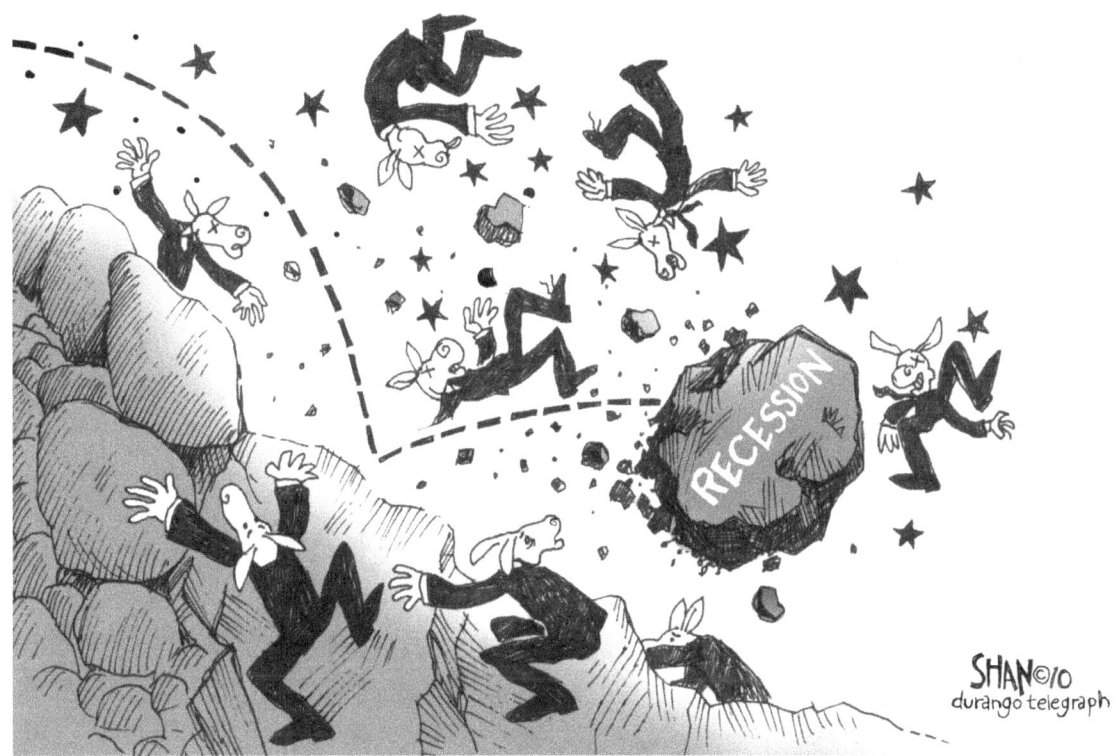

As promised by the polls and anyone paying the least bit of attention, the 2010 mid-terms went down as a historic political reversal. 61 House seats changed hands, giving the GOP a strong majority. Several Governorships also went red, as did many state houses. Republican candidates won handily at the local level and came within a few seats of the majority in the Senate.

Also as expected, the regressives almost immediately began to overplay their hand. Prominent members of the Senate called for a new war with Iran, and Mitch McConnell, the Senate Minority Leader, stated bluntly that his main goal was to make Obama a one term president.

Obama took responsibility for the "shellacking," and offered more compromise in the future.

At first blush, the overturn seems to be a response to Democratic ineptitude, even though the economy was stabilized and growing by 2010. Yet people did not feel the growth as joblessness was still high. My take is that the twin demons of the worst economic collapse since the great depression, and Obama's unwillingness to assign blame for the debacle in any public way, (unlike FDR, who held high profile hearings into banking as the first order of business), allowed a "villain vacuum." The GOP was only too happy to insert the Dems and the President into the slot.

All this adds up to a cautionary tale for readers of this humble volume. American democracy can change dramatically. It is those that desire change the most who will prevail.

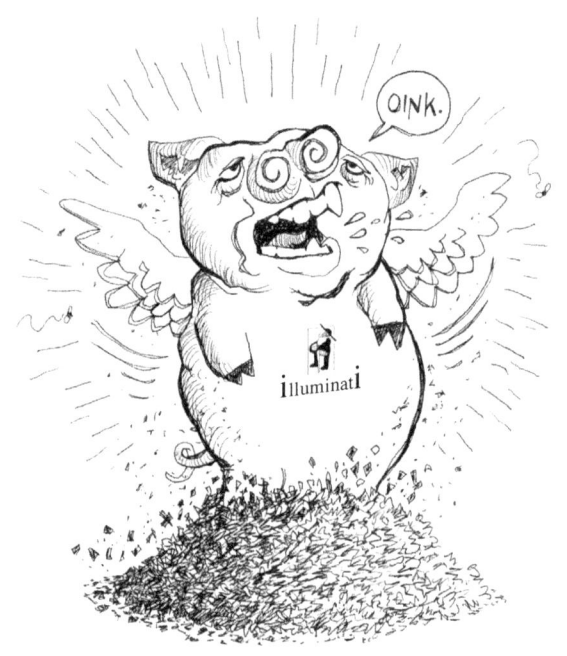

www.ingramcontent.com/pod-product-compliance
Lightning Source LLC
Chambersburg PA
CBHW081131170526
45165CB00008B/2636